FLASHMAPS!

THE INSTANT GUIDE TO

W9-DGG-105

Washington

The idea of SINGLE SUBJECT MAPS with related material was conceived by FLASHMAPS Publications in 1967. A single-subject map, color-coded and cross-indexed, has proven to be a useful tool for clearly dispensing information. FLASHMAPS INSTANT GUIDE books are used by both natives and visitors alike to save time, money and energy.

ENJOY WASHINGTON!

RANDOM HOUSE
NEW YORK

EDITOR:
  Toy Lasker
CARTOGRAPHERS:
  Timothy W. Lasker
  Sally Jarman
DIRECTOR of RESEARCH:
  Gladys F. Caterinicchio

© **1975 Flashmaps Publications, Inc.**
Revised 1977, 79, 80, 81, 83, 85, 86, 87, 89

Library of Congress Card No. 75-6206
ISBN 0-942226-33-X
Manufactured in The United States of America

CONTENTS

IMPORTANT TELEPHONE NUMBERS
(MD Area 301) (DC Area Code 202) (VA Area 703)
EMERGENCIES

Police	911	U.S. Secret Service	634-5100
Fire & Rescue	911	U.S. Park Police	426-6600
Ambulance	911	Alcohol/Drug Hotline	727-0474
Police Dept Information	**727-4326**	**DC Hotline**	**223-2255**
Fire Dept Headquarters	**462-1762**	**VD Hotline**	**832-7000**
Poison Control Center	**625-3333**	**Animal Bites**	**576-6665**
Suicide Hotline	**362-8100**	**Deaf Emergency**	**727-9334**
Children's Protection	**727-0995**	**Water & Sewer**	**673-6600**
Civil Defense	**727-6161**	**DC General Hospital**	**675-5000**
Coast Guard	**267-2229**	**Tipster's Confidential**	**393-2222**
FBI	**324-3000**	**Rape & Assault**	**333-7273**

RECORDED INFORMATION

Daily Tourist Info	737-8866	National Archives	523-3000
Dial-A-Museum	357-2020	Passport Office Info	783-8200
Dial-A-Park	485-7275	Ticketron	659-2601
Dial-A-Phenomenon	737-8855	Time of Day	844-2525
Dial-A-Prayer	347-4341	Weather	936-1212
DC Recreation Dept	673-7660	U.S. Weather	936-1212

SERVICES

Abandoned Auto Disposal	673-6993	Marriage License	879-2839
Aging	724-5626	Medicaid	724-5173
Air Pollution	426-2675	Metrorail & Metrobus Info	637-7000
Business Information	637-7000	Metrobus Lost Property	962-1195
Consumer Complaints	727-7065	Motor Vehicles	727-6680
DC Government	727-1000	National Parks	343-1100
Federal Info	647-4000	Planned Parenthood	347-8500
Food Stamps	727-0858	Telegrams	737-4260
Garbage & Trash	727-4825	Travelers' Aid	347-0101
Human Services	724-5466	US Capitol	224-3121
Income Tax—DC	727-6103	US Postal Service	682-9595
Federal	488-3100	White House Tour Info	456-7041
IVIS Translation Service	783-6540	Zoo Information	673-4800

AIRLINES INTO NATIONAL & DULLES AIRPORTS

Aeroflot	429-4922	Lufthansa	*645-3880
Air France	*237-2747	Midway	*621-5700
Alaska Air	*426-0333	Midwest Air Express	*452-2022
All Nippon Air	*235-9262	Northwest	737-7333
Allegheny Commuter	*428-4253	Pan American	845-8000
American	393-2345	Piedmont	620-0400
American Eagle	393-2345	Piedmont-Henson	620-5350
Braniff	*272-6433	Presidential Airways	478-9700
British Airways	*247-9297	Saudi Arabian Air	333-3800
Continental	478-9700	TWA	737-7400
Delta	468-2282	United	893-3400
Eastern	393-4000	US Air	783-4500
Jet American Air	*421-7574	Wings	*648-9464

TERMINALS

Andrews AFB	981-3528	**Dulles Wash Airport**	471-4242
Balt-Wash Airport	(301) 261-1000	**Wash National Air**	(703) 685-8000
AMTRAK		Union Station	*USA-RAIL
Gray Line Tours		4th & E St SW	(301) 386-8300
Greyhound/Trailways Bus Terminal		1110 New York Ave NW	565-2662
Tourmobile		1000 Ohio Dr SW	554-7950

4   *(800) Toll Free

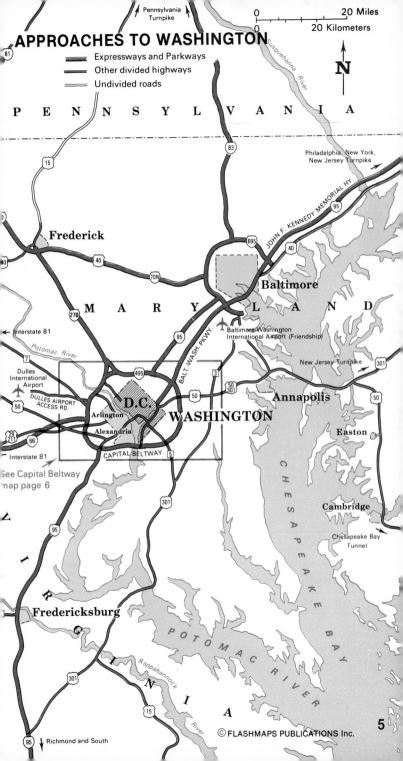

APPROACHES TO WASHINGTON

▬▬	Expressways and Parkways
▬▬	Other divided highways
══	Undivided roads

0 · 20 Miles
0 · 20 Kilometers

N

Pennsylvania Turnpike

Susquehanna River

P E N N S Y L V A N I A

Philadelphia, New York, New Jersey Turnpike

JOHN F. KENNEDY MEMORIAL HY.

Frederick

Baltimore

M A R Y L A N D

← Interstate 81

Potomac River

Baltimore-Washington International Airport (Friendship)

Dulles International Airport

New Jersey Turnpike →

DULLES AIRPORT ACCESS RD.

D.C.

WASHINGTON

Annapolis

Arlington

Easton

Alexandria

← Interstate 81

CAPITAL BELTWAY

See Capital Beltway map page 6

C H E S A P E A K E   B A Y

Cambridge

Chesapeake Bay Tunnel

V I R G I N I A

Fredericksburg

P O T O M A C   R I V E R

Rappahannock River

↓ Richmond and South

5

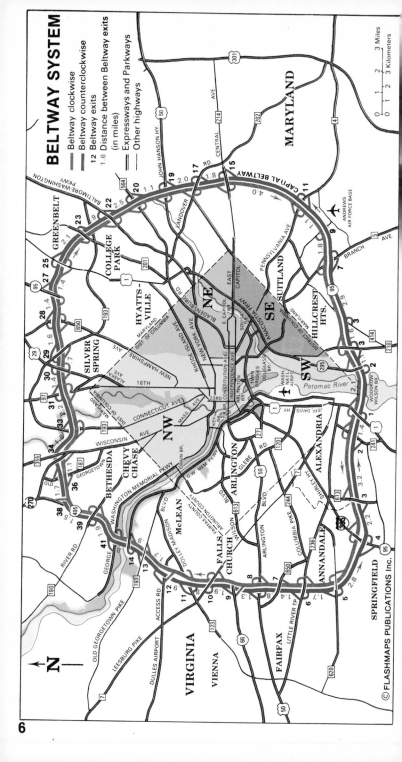

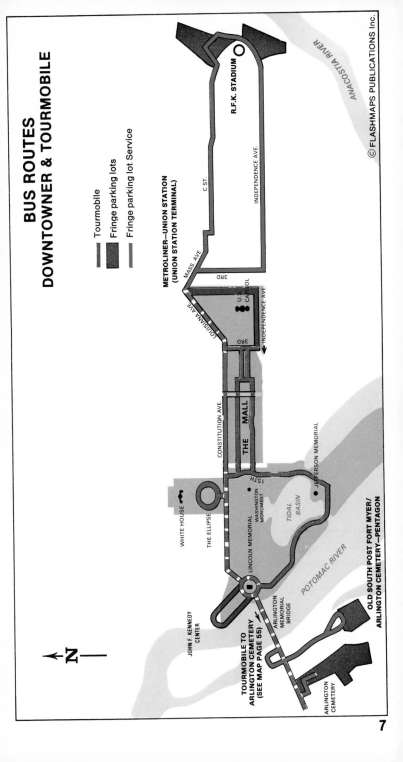

BUS ROUTES
DOWNTOWNER & TOURMOBILE

Tourmobile
Fringe parking lots
Fringe parking lot Service

METROLINER—UNION STATION
(UNION STATION TERMINAL)

R.F.K. STADIUM

ANACOSTIA RIVER

C ST.

MASS. AVE.

INDEPENDENCE AVE.

3RD

LOUISIANA AVE.

U.S. CAPITOL

INDEPENDENCE AVE.

3RD

CONSTITUTION AVE.

THE MALL

WHITE HOUSE

THE ELLIPSE

15TH

WASHINGTON MONUMENT

TIDAL BASIN

JEFFERSON MEMORIAL

LINCOLN MEMORIAL

POTOMAC RIVER

JOHN F. KENNEDY CENTER

ARLINGTON MEMORIAL BRIDGE

TOURMOBILE TO ARLINGTON CEMETERY
(SEE MAP PAGE 55)

OLD SOUTH POST FORT MYER/
ARLINGTON CEMETERY—PENTAGON

ARLINGTON CEMETERY

© FLASHMAPS PUBLICATIONS Inc.

N

7

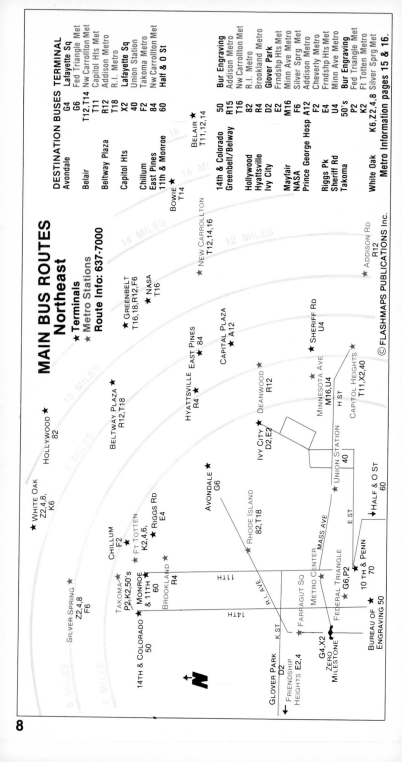

MAIN BUS ROUTES
Northeast

★ Terminals
★ Metro Stations
Route Info: 637-7000

DESTINATION	BUSES	TERMINAL
Avondale	G4	Lafayette Sq
	G6	Fed Triangle Met
Belair	T12,T14	Nw Carrollton Met
	T11	Capitol Hts Met
Beltway Plaza	R12	Addison Metro
	T18	R.I. Metro
Capitol Hts	X2	Lafayette Sq
	40	Union Station
Chillum	F2	Takoma Metro
East Pines	84	Nw Carrollton Met
11th & Monroe	60	Half & O St
Bur Engraving	50	Addison Metro
14th & Colorado	R15	Nw Carrollton Met
Greenbelt/Belway	T16	R.I. Metro
		Brookland Metro
Hollywood	82	Glover Park
Hyattsville	R4	Frndshp Hts Met
Ivy City	D2	Minn Ave Metro
	E2	Silver Sprg Met
Mayfair	M16	Addison Metro
NASA	F6	Cheverly Metro
Prince George Hosp	A12	Frndshp Hts Met
	F2	Minn Ave Metro
Riggs Pk	E4	
Sheriff Rd	U4	Bur Engraving
Takoma	50's	P2	Fed Triangle Met
		Ft Totten Metro
White Oak	K6,Z2,4,8	Silver Sprg Met

Metro Information pages 15 & 16.

© FLASHMAPS PUBLICATIONS Inc.

★ BELAIR
T11,12,14

BOWIE
T14

NEW CARROLLTON
T12,14,16

★ GREENBELT
T16,18,R12,F6

★ NASA
T16

ADDISON RD
R12

★ HOLLYWOOD
82

★ WHITE OAK
Z2,4,8,
K6

★ BELTWAY PLAZA
R12,T18

★ CAPITAL PLAZA
A12

★ HYATTSVILLE
R4

EAST PINES
84

★ DEANWOOD
R12

★ SHERIFF RD
U4

SILVER SPRING
Z2,4,6

★ CHILLUM
F2

★ TAKOMA
P2,K2,50's

MONROE
& 11TH
60

★ FT TOTTEN
K2,4,6,

RIGGS RD
E4

BROOKLAND
R4

★ AVONDALE
G6

★ IVY CITY
D2,E2

★ MINNESOTA AVE
M16,U4

H ST

CAPITOL HEIGHTS
T11,X2,40

RHODE ISLAND
82,T18

UNION STATION
40

MASS AVE

E ST

★ HALF & O ST
60

14TH & COLORADO
50

★ GLOVER PARK
D2

FRIENDSHIP
HEIGHTS E2,4

K ST

11TH

14TH

FARRAGUT SQ

METRO CENTER

FEDERAL TRIANGLE

10 TH & PENN
70

G4,X2
ZERO
MILESTONE

G6,P2

R.I. AVE

★ BUREAU OF
ENGRAVING 50

8

MAIN BUS ROUTES
Southeast

★ Terminals
★ Metro Stations

Route Info: 637-7000

DESTINATION	BUSES	TERMINAL
Andrews AFB	J12	Addison Metro
	K12	Potomac Metro
Bellevue	A4	Archives
Capitol Heights	40	Union Station
Congress Heights	A2	Archives
District Heights	V12	Potomac Metro
	J12	Addison Metro
DC General	96	McLean Gardens
Fairfax Village	K12,W6	Potomac Metro
	V12	Addison Metro
Garfield	92	Duke Ellington Brdg
Hillcrest	36	Friendship Hts Metro
Livingston	A6,A8	Archives
Marlow Hgts	D12	Federal Ctr Metro
	C12,C14	Potomac Metro
Minnesota Ave	V6	Bur Engraving
Naylor Garden	34	Friendship Hts Metro
Oxon Hill	W12	Federal Ctr Metro
Ridge Rd	V4	Bur Engraving
RFKStadium/Armory	42	Mt. Pleasant
Shipley Terrace	32	Friendship Hts Metro
Stanton Rd	94	Duke Ellington Bridge
Temple Hill	H12	Potomac Metro

Metro Information pages 15 & 16.

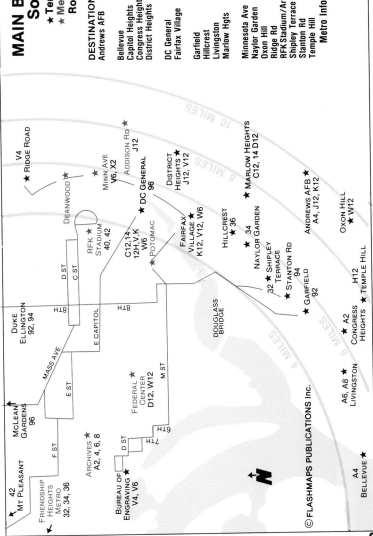

© FLASHMAPS PUBLICATIONS Inc.

9

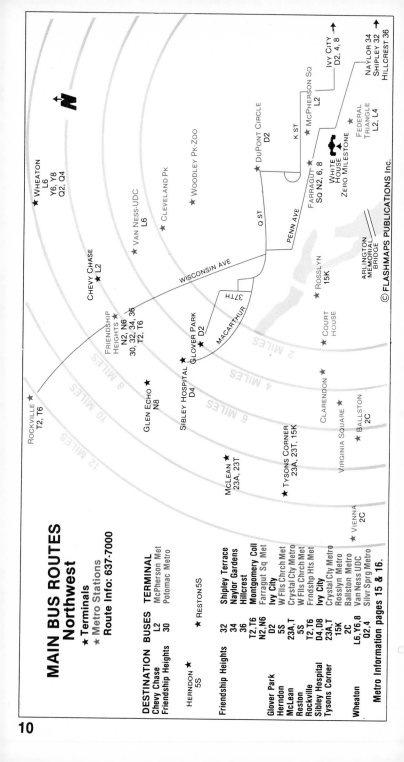

MAIN BUS ROUTES
Northwest

★ Terminals
★ Metro Stations
Route Info: 637-7000

DESTINATION	BUSES	TERMINAL
Chevy Chase	L2	McPherson Met
Friendship Heights	30	Potomac Metro

★ HERNDON
5S

★ RESTON 5S

	DESTINATION	BUSES	TERMINAL
Friendship Heights	Shipley Terrace	32	
	Naylor Gardens	34	
	Hillcrest	36	
	Montgomery Coll	T2, T6	
	Ivy City	N2, N6	
Glover Park	Farragut Sq Met	D2	
Herndon	W Flls Chrch Met	5S	
McLean	Crystal Cty Metro	23A, T	
Reston	W Flls Chrch Met	5S	
Rockville	Frndshp Hts Met	T2, T6	
Sibley Hospital	Ivy City	D4, D8	
Tysons Corner	Crystal Cty Metro	23A, T	
	Rosslyn Metro	15K	
	Ballston Metro	2C	
Wheaton	Van Ness UDC	L6, Y6, 8	
	Silvr Sprg Metro	Q2, 4	

Metro Information pages 15 & 16.

© FLASHMAPS PUBLICATIONS Inc.

N

★ WHEATON L6 Y6, Y8 Q2, Q4

★ CHEVY CHASE L2

ROCKVILLE T2, T6

WISCONSIN AVE

FRIENDSHIP HEIGHTS
30, 32, 34, 36
N2, N6
T2, T6

★ GLEN ECHO N8

★ SIBLEY HOSPITAL D4

★ GLOVER PARK D2

MACARTHUR

37TH

Q ST

PENN AVE

★ VAN NESS-UDC L6

★ CLEVELAND PK

★ WOODLEY PK-ZOO

★ DUPONT CIRCLE D2

K ST

★ MCPHERSON SQ L2

IVY CITY D2, 4, 8

★ FARRAGUT SQ N2, 6, 8

WHITE HOUSE
ZERO MILESTONE

FEDERAL TRIANGLE L2, L4

NAYLOR 34
SHIPLEY 32
HILLCREST 36

ARLINGTON MEMORIAL BRIDGE

★ ROSSLYN 15K

★ COURT HOUSE

★ CLARENDON

★ VIRGINIA SQUARE

★ BALLSTON 2C

★ MCLEAN 23A, 23T

★ TYSONS CORNER 23A, 23T, 15K

★ VIENNA 2C

2 MILES
4 MILES
6 MILES
8 MILES
10 MILES
12 MILES

10

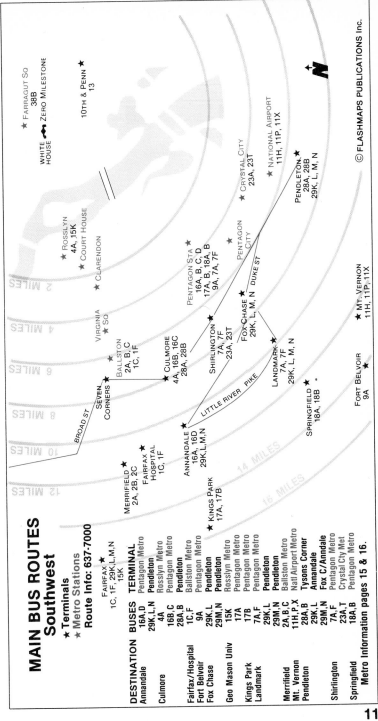

MAIN BUS ROUTES
Southwest

★ Terminals
★ Metro Stations
Route Info: 637-7000

DESTINATION	BUSES	TERMINAL
Annandale	16A,D	Pentagon Metro
	29K,L,N	Pendleton
Culmore	4A	Rosslyn Metro
	16B,C	Pentagon Metro
	28A,B	Pendleton
Fairfax/Hospital	1C,F	Ballston Metro
Fort Belvoir	9A	Pentagon Metro
Fox Chase	29K,L	Pendleton
	29M,N	Pendleton
Geo Mason Univ	15K	Rosslyn Metro
Kings Park	17A	Pentagon Metro
	17B	Pentagon Metro
Landmark	7A,F	Pentagon Metro
	29K,L	Pendleton
	29M,N	Pendleton
Merrifield	2A,B,C	Ballston Metro
	11H,P,X	Natl Airport Metro
Mt. Vernon	28A,B	Tysons Corner
	29K,L	Annandale
Pendleton	29M,N	Fox C/Anndale
	7A,F	Pentagon Metro
Shirlington	23A,T	Crystal Cty Met
Springfield	18A,B	Pentagon Metro

Metro Information pages 15 & 16.

★ FARRAGUT SQ 38B
WHITE HOUSE ⬥ ZERO MILESTONE
10TH & PENN 13

★ ROSSLYN 4A, 15K
★ COURT HOUSE
★ CLARENDON

★ VIRGINIA SQ

★ BALLSTON 2A, B, C 1C, 1F
★ CULMORE 4A, 16B, 16C 28A, 28B

SEVEN CORNERS
BROAD ST

★ MERRIFIELD 2A, 2B, 2C
★ FAIRFAX HOSPITAL 1C, 1F

★ FAIRFAX 1C, 1F, 29K,L,M,N 15K

★ PENTAGON STA 16A, B, C, D 17A, B, 18A, B 9A, 7A, 7F
★ PENTAGON CITY
★ CRYSTAL CITY 23A, 23T
★ NATIONAL AIRPORT 11H, 11P, 11X

FOX CHASE 29K, L, M, N DUKE ST
★ SHIRLINGTON 7A, 7F 23A, 23T
★ LANDMARK 7A, 7F 29K, L, M, N
LITTLE RIVER PIKE
★ ANNANDALE 16A, 16D 29K,L,M,N
★ KINGS PARK 17A, 17B
★ SPRINGFIELD 18A, 18B
★ FORT BELVOIR 9A
★ MT. VERNON 11H, 11P, 11X

★ PENDLETON 28A, 28B 29K, L, M, N

2 MILES 4 MILES 6 MILES 8 MILES 10 MILES 12 MILES 14 MILES 16 MILES

N

© FLASHMAPS PUBLICATIONS Inc.

11

METRO BUS & RAIL TO IMPORTANT CENTERS

Center	Bus Route	Map Pg	Metro	Metro Stop
Carter Barron Amph	5's	10	Red	Silver Spring
Catholic Univ	80, 81, H2, H4	8	Red	Brookland
Chevy Chase Mazza	T6,30's, N2, N6	10	Red	Friendship Hgts
Convention Center	60, 70, K4	8	Blue/Red/Orn	Metro Center
Crystal City	none	11	Blue	Crystal City
DC Armory	42, 96	9	Blue/Orange	Stadium/Armory
Gallaudet College	92,94,D2,D4,D8	8		
Greyhound	60,K4,D2,D4,D8	9	Blue/Org/Red	Metro Center
Hospitals:				
Capitol Hill	92,94	8	Blue/Orange	Capitol South
Childrens	H2, H4	10	Red	Brookland
Columbia	30's	10	Blue/Orange	Foggy Bottom
DC General	96,98,B2,B4,B5	9	Red/Orange	Stdium/Armory
Fairfax	1C,1F,26T	11	Orange	Ballston
Georgetown Univ	D4	10	Red	DuPont Circle
Geo Washington U	30's	10	Blue/Orange	Foggy Bottom
Hadley	A4	11	Blue/Orange	Federal Center
Howard Univ	70's,G2	8	Red	Gallery/DuPont Circle
Prince George	A12,F2	8	Orange	Landover/Cheverly
Providence	80, 81	8	Red	Brookland
Psychiatric Instit	D4	10	Red	Dupont Circle
St. Elizabeth's	A's	9	Blue/Orange	Federal Center
Southeast Comm	A2	9	Blue/Orange	Federal Center
Sibley	D4	10	Red	DuPont Circle
Walter Reed	S2, S4, 70's	8	Red	Silver Spring
Washington Center	H2, H4	8	Red	Brookland
V.A.	H2, H4	8	Red	Brookland
Howard University	70's, G2	8	Red	Gallery/DuPont
Ivy City	D2, D4, E2	8	Red	Union Sta/Ft Totten
Kennedy Center	46,81	10	Red	DuPont Circ/Metro Ctr
Landmark	29K, L, M, N	11	Yellow	King Street
Landover Mall	A12	8	Orange	Landover
Marine Barracks	52,54,92,94	9	Blue/Orange	East Market
Montgomery Mall	J2, J3	10	Red	Medical Center
NASA Greenbelt	T16	11	Orange	New Carrollton
National Airport	11H, 11P, 11X	11	Blue/Yellow	National Airport
National Shrine	80,81,H2/4G4/6	8	Red	Brookland
Naval Observatory	N2, N4, N6	10	Red	DuPont Circle
Naval Ordinance Lab	K6	8	Red	Brookland
Naval Research Lab	A4, A5	9	Blue/Orange	Federal Center
Navy Annex	16's	11	Blue/Yellow	Pentagon
Navy Yard	52,54,92,94,	9	Blue/Orange	East Market
Pentagon	16's, 17's,8's	11	Blue/Yellow	Pentagon
Prince George Plaza	F4, F6, R2	8	Red	Silver Spr/Brklnd
RFK Stadium	42, 96	9	Blue/Orange	Stadium/Armory
Reston, VA	5's	10	Orange	West Falls Church
Seven Corners	1's	10	Orange	Ballston
Springfield	18's, 26T	11	Blue/Orge	Pentagon/Dunn Loring
Trailways Bus	96	9	Red	Union Station
Tysons Corner	5S, 28A & B	10	Orange	West Falls Church
Union Station	40, 42, D's, 96	8	Red	Union Station
Univ of DC	L2, L4, L6	8	Red	Van Ness
Univ Maryland	82,83,R2	8	Red	Brookland/R.I.
Washington Cathedral	30's, N2, N6	10	Red	Friendship Heights
White Flint	70's, G2	10	Red	White Flint
Zoo	L's	10	Red	Woodley Pk Zoo

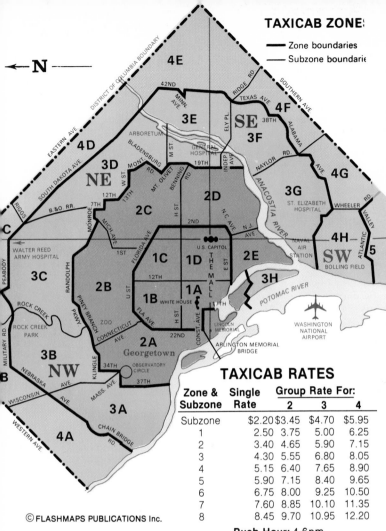

TAXICAB ZONES

— Zone boundaries
— Subzone boundaries

← N →

4E

4F

SE

3E

3F

4D

42ND

MINN. AVE

RIDGE RD

TEXAS AVE

SOUTHERN AVE

38TH

ALABAMA

ELY PL

ARBORETUM

M ST

GENERAL HOSPITAL

19TH

NAYLOR RD

4G

3D

NE

BLADENSBURG RD

MONT. RD

MT. OLIVET RD

BENNING RD

N.C. AVE

3G

ST. ELIZABETH HOSPITAL

WHEELER RD

EASTERN AVE

SOUTH DAKOTA AVE

RIGGS

12TH

B & O. RR.

7TH

13TH

MONROE

MICH. AVE

2C

2D

H ST

2ND

INDEP. AVE

ANACOSTIA RIVER

VALLEY RD

C

WALTER REED ARMY HOSPITAL

1ST

FLORIDA AVE

U.S. CAPITOL

E ST

NJ AVE

NAVAL AIR STATION

4H

5

1C

1D

THE MALL

2E

SW

BOLLING FIELD

ATLANTIC

3C

PEABODY

RANDOLPH

PINEY BRANCH PKWY

12TH

U ST

CONNECTICUT AVE

ZOO

2B

1B

WHITE HOUSE

1A

17TH

3H

POTOMAC RIVER

WASHINGTON NATIONAL AIRPORT

ROCK CREEK PARK

ROCK CREEK

FLA AVE

H ST

CONST. AVE

22ND

LINCOLN MEMORIAL

MILITARY RD

3B

NW

NEBRASKA AVE

KLINGLE

34TH

OBSERVATORY CIRCLE

2A

Georgetown

ARLINGTON MEMORIAL BRIDGE

WISCONSIN AVE

MASS. AVE

37TH

B

3A

WESTERN AVE

4A

CHAIN BRIDGE RD

DISTRICT OF COLUMBIA BOUNDARY

© FLASHMAPS PUBLICATIONS Inc.

TAXICAB RATES

Zone & Subzone	Single Rate	Group Rate For:		
		2	3	4
Subzone	$2.20	$3.45	$4.70	$5.95
1	2.50	3.75	5.00	6.25
2	3.40	4.65	5.90	7.15
3	4.30	5.55	6.80	8.05
4	5.15	6.40	7.65	8.90
5	5.90	7.15	8.40	9.65
6	6.75	8.00	9.25	10.50
7	7.60	8.85	10.10	11.35
8	8.45	9.70	10.95	12.20

Rush Hour: 4-6pm
$1.00 surcharge.

Rates change between zones and subzones.
Two or more passengers:
 Same destination—group rate
 Different destination—single rate
 Children five and under: no charge
Airport Fare: Dulles—$27.00 to $35.00   International—$6.00 to $9.00
 Luggage: One piece free per person. 15¢ each additional.
Telephone called taxi: $1.00 extra.
Messenger service: Same rate as single passenger.
Trunks: in excess of 34'' x 18'' x 9'' or three cubic feet—$1.25 each.
Waiting rate: 75¢ for each 5 minutes up to 45 minutes.
Hourly rate: First hour or fraction thereof: $12.00
 Additional 15 minutes—$3.00
Handicapped passengers: No extra charge for aids or Seeing Eye dogs.

13

METRO STATIONS—ALPHABETICAL

Metro Stop	Approximate Location	Metro Line	Fringe Parking
Addison Road	Central Ave Addison Rd, MD	**Blue**	551
Archives	Penn Ave & 7th NW, DC	**Yellow**	
Arlington Cemetery*	Memorial Dr & Jeff Davis, VA	**Blue**	
Ballston*	Fairfax Blvd & N Stuart St, VA	**Orange**	
Benning Rd	E Capitol & Benning Rd NE, DC	**Blue**	
Bethesda	Wisconsin at Montgomery Ln, MD	**Red**	
Braddock Rd	Braddock Rd & West St, VA	**Yellow**	
Brookland-CUA	Michigan Av & Bunker Hill Rd N-E, DC	**Red**	
Capitol Heights	E Capitol & Southern Ave, MD	**Blue**	336
Capitol South	1st St betw C / D Sts SE, DC	**Blue/Orange**	
Cheverly	Columbia Pk Rd & Cheverly, MD	**Orange**	496 & Midday
Clarendon*	Wilson Blvd & N Highland St, VA	**Orange**	
Cleveland Park*	Porter/Ordway & Conn, DC	**Red**	
Court House*	Wilson Blvd / Uhle St, VA	**Orange**	
Crystal City*	18th St betw Clark & Jeff Davis, VA	**Blue/Yellow**	
Deanwood	Minn Ave betw Nash & 48th St, MD	**Orange**	191 & Midday
Dunn Loring*	Gallows Rd & I-66, VA	**Orange**	1050
Dupont Circle*	Conn & Q / 19th St, DC	**Red**	
Eastern Market*	Penn Ave & 7th St SE, DC	**Blue/Orange**	
Eisenhower Ave	Eisenhower Ave & RR Sta, VA	**Yellow**	
Falls Church, East*	I-66 N Sycamore St, VA	**Orange**	365
Falls Church, West*	I-66 at Leesburg Pke VA	**Orange**	1000
Farragut North*	Conn & L/Conn & K Sts NW, DC	**Red**	
Farragut West*	Eye & 17th /Eye & 18th Sts, DC	**Blue/Orange**	
Federal Center*	D St & 3rd, DC	**Blue/Orange**	
Federal Triangle*	12th & Penn / Constitution, DC	**Blue/Orange**	
Foggy Bottom(GWU)*	Eye St & 23rd NW, DC	**Blue/Orange**	
Fort Totten	Galloway St at RR, DC	**Red**	330 & Midday
Friendship Heights	Western Ave & Wisconsin, DC	**Red**	
Gallery Place*	7th & G/7th & H/ 9th & G NW	**Red/Yellow**	
Grosvenor	Rockville Pke & Grosvenor, MD	**Red**	614
Huntington	Huntington Ave & Kings Hwy, VA	**Yellow**	2282
Judiciary Square*	F & 4th - 5th/D-E & 4th, NW	**Red**	
King Street	King St & Commonwealth, VA	**Yellow**	
Landover	Penn Dr & N of Landover, MD	**Orange**	1131 & Midday
L'Enfant Plaza*	D & 9th/D & 6-7th/Md & 7th, SW	**Blu/Or/Yell**	
McPherson Square*	Eye & 14th/Vermont & Eye, DC	**Blue/Orange**	
Medical Center*	Rockville Pike & South Dr, MD	**Red**	
Metro Center*	G & 11th, 12th, 13th, F & 12th	**Red/Blu/Orng**	
Minnesota Ave	Minn & Grant St NE, DC	**Orange**	263 & Midday
National Airport	North Term & Smith Blvd, VA	**Blue/Yellow**	
New Carrollton	79th Ave & RR Sta, MD	**Orange**	1552 & Midday
Pentagon*	Pentagon concourse/Metrobus ls, VA	**Blue/Yellow**	
Pentagon City*	Hayes Rd betw Army/Navy & 15th, VA	**Blue/Yellow**	800 (private)
Potomac Ave*	14th St & Potomac Ave SE	**Blue/Orange**	
Rhode Island Ave	Rl Ave & 8th St NE (RR Sta), DC	**Red**	322 & Midday
Rockville	Hungerford Dr (355) & Park Rd, MD	**Red**	518
Rosslyn*	N Moore St & 19th / Wilson, VA	**Blue/Orange**	
Shady Grove	Rt 355 & Redland Rd, MD	**Red**	3149
Silver Spring	Colesville betw E/W hwy & Wayne, Md	**Red**	537
Smithsonian*	12th & Indep/12th & Jefferson, SW	**Blue/Orange**	
Stadium Armory*	19th St & C/19th & Indep, SE	**Blue/Orange**	2000 (stadium)
Takoma	Carroll Ave & Cedar St NW, DC	**Red**	100 & Midday
Tenleytown	Wisconsin & Albermarle Av NW, DC	**Red**	
Twinbrook	Halpine Rd & RR Sta, MD	**Red**	
UDC-Van Ness	Van Ness & Conn NW, DC	**Red**	
Union Station*	Union Station (1st & Mass), NE	**Red**	
Vienna*	Nutley St & I-66, VA	**Orange**	2135
Virginia Square*	Fairfax & N Monroe, VA	**Orange**	
White Flint	Marinelli Rd & Rockville Pke, MD	**Red**	933
Zoological Park	Conn & 24th/Woodley NW, DC	**Red**	

*Underground station with elevator   **Midday parking: 10 AM to 3 PM**

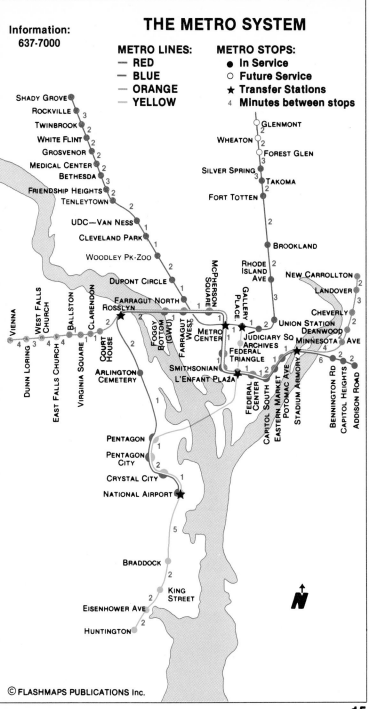

THE METRO SYSTEM

Information:
637-7000

METRO LINES:
— RED
— BLUE
— ORANGE
— YELLOW

METRO STOPS:
● In Service
○ Future Service
★ Transfer Stations
4 Minutes between stops

SHADY GROVE
ROCKVILLE 3
TWINBROOK 2
WHITE FLINT 2
GROSVENOR 2
MEDICAL CENTER 2
BETHESDA 2
FRIENDSHIP HEIGHTS 2
TENLEYTOWN 2
UDC—VAN NESS 1
CLEVELAND PARK 1
WOODLEY PK-ZOO 2
DUPONT CIRCLE 1
FARRAGUT NORTH
ROSSLYN 2

GLENMONT
WHEATON 2
FOREST GLEN 3
SILVER SPRING 3
TAKOMA 2
FORT TOTTEN 2
BROOKLAND 2
RHODE ISLAND AVE 3
McPHERSON SQUARE
GALLERY PLACE
NEW CARROLLTON
LANDOVER 2
CHEVERLY 3
UNION STATION 2
DEANWOOD
MINNESOTA AVE 2
BENNINGTON RD 6
CAPITOL HEIGHTS 2
ADDISON ROAD

VIENNA 4
DUNN LORING 4
WEST FALLS CHURCH 3
EAST FALLS CHURCH 1
BALLSTON 2
VIRGINIA SQUARE
CLARENDON 1
COURT HOUSE 2
ARLINGTON CEMETERY

FARRAGUT WEST 1
FOGGY BOTTOM (GWU)
METRO CENTER 1
JUDICIARY SQ 1
ARCHIVES
FEDERAL TRIANGLE 1
SMITHSONIAN
L'ENFANT PLAZA
FEDERAL CENTER
CAPITOL SOUTH
EASTERN MARKET 1
POTOMAC AVE
STADIUM ARMORY 4

PENTAGON 1
PENTAGON CITY 2
CRYSTAL CITY 1
NATIONAL AIRPORT

5

BRADDOCK 2
KING STREET 2
EISENHOWER AVE 2
HUNTINGTON

N

© FLASHMAPS PUBLICATIONS Inc.

15

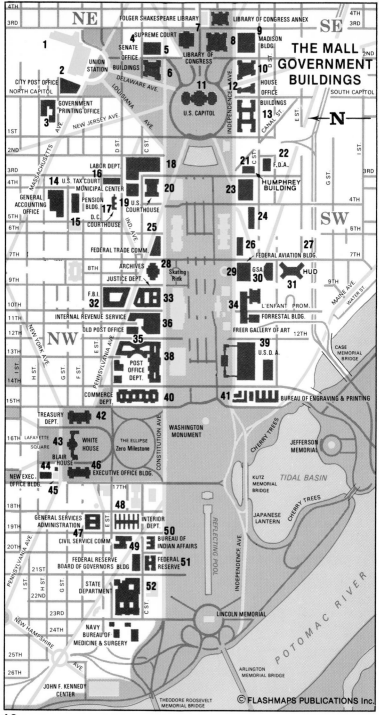

THE MALL
GOVERNMENT
BUILDINGS

N

© FLASHMAPS PUBLICATIONS Inc.

NE **SE** **SW** **NW**

1

2

City Post Office

3 Government Printing Office

4 Senate Office Buildings

Union Station

Folger Shakespeare Library

Supreme Court

5

6

7 Library of Congress

Library of Congress Annex

8

9 Madison Bldg.

10

11 U.S. Capitol

12

13 House Office Buildings

14 U.S. Tax Court

General Accounting Office

Labor Dept. 16

Municipal Center

15 Pension Bldg. 17

19 U.S. Courthouse

D.C. Courthouse

18

20

21

22 F.D.A.

23 Humphrey Building

24

25

Federal Trade Comm.

26

27

Federal Aviation Bldg.

29 GSA 30

31 HUD

28 Skating Rink

Archives

Justice Dept.

F.B.I. 32

33

Internal Revenue Service

34 L'Enfant Prom.

Forrestal Bldg.

36

Old Post Office 35

38

Post Office Dept.

Freer Gallery of Art

39 U.S.D.A.

Commerce Dept. 40

41 Bureau of Engraving & Printing

Treasury Dept. 42

43 White House

Blair House

44

45 New Exec. Office Bldg.

46 Executive Office Bldg.

Lafayette Square

The Ellipse
Zero Milestone

Washington Monument

Constitution Ave.

Reflecting Pool

Jefferson Memorial

Tidal Basin

Kutz Memorial Bridge

Japanese Lantern

Cherry Trees

Case Memorial Bridge

48

General Services Administration 47

Interior Dept.

Civil Service Comm.

50 Bureau of Indian Affairs

49

Federal Reserve Board of Governors Bldg.

51 Federal Reserve

52 State Department

Navy Bureau of Medicine & Surgery

Lincoln Memorial

Arlington Memorial Bridge

Theodore Roosevelt Memorial Bridge

John F. Kennedy Center

Potomac River

MALL GOVERNMENT BUILDINGS—BY MAP NUMBER

MALL GOVERNMENT BUILDINGS—ALPHABETICAL

ARCHITECTURAL LANDMARKS

Building	Architect	Date	Map Page
Arts & Industries	Cluss & Schultze	1880	18
Blair—Lee House	Unknown	1824	16
Botanical Gardens	Bennett, Parson, Frost	1902	18
Bureau of Engraving	James G. Hill	1880	16
Capitol	Wm. Thornton & Latrobe	1829	16
Constitution Hall	John Russell Pope	1930	18
Corcoran Gallery of Art	Ernest Flagg	1897	18
Decatur House	Benjamin Latrobe	1818	18
DC Courthouse	George Hadfield	1850	16
DC Government Building	Cope & Stewardson	1908	16
Dulles Internat'l Airport	Eero Saarinen	1962	5
Executive Office	A. B. Mullett	1888	16
Hirshhorn Museum	Gordon Bundshaft	1974	18
John F Kennedy Center	Edward Durell Stone	1969	18

(Continued) **17**

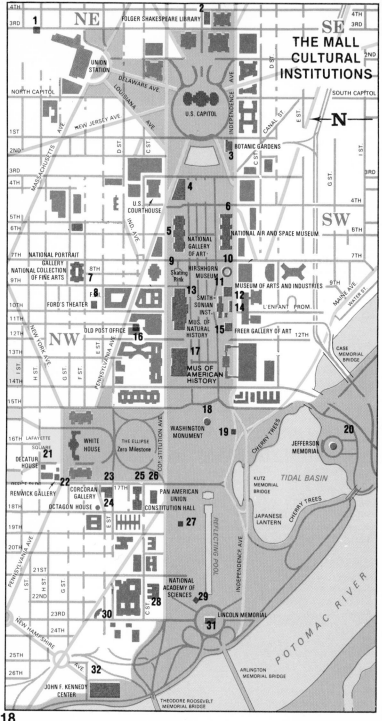

THE MALL
CULTURAL
INSTITUTIONS

NE

SE

SW

NW

N

1

2

Folger Shakespeare Library

4TH
3RD
2ND

4TH
3RD

UNION STATION

DELAWARE AVE.

LOUISIANA AVE.

NORTH CAPITOL

MASSACHUSETTS AVE.

NEW JERSEY AVE.

U.S. CAPITOL

SOUTH CAPITOL

CANAL ST.

D ST.

E ST.

1ST

2ND

3RD
4TH

3 Botanic Gardens

C ST.

1ST

3RD

4 U.S. COURTHOUSE

4TH

D ST.

C ST.

IND. AVE.

5TH
6TH

6 NATIONAL AIR AND SPACE MUSEUM

5TH
6TH

5

NATIONAL GALLERY OF ART

7TH National Portrait Gallery

NATIONAL COLLECTION OF FINE ARTS

7

9 Skating Rink

HIRSHHORN MUSEUM

10

9TH

8TH

7TH

8

Ford's Theater

13 SMITHSONIAN INST.

Museum of Arts and Industries

12

14

L'ENFANT PROM.

9TH

MAINE AVE.

WATER ST.

10TH

OLD POST OFFICE

16

MUS. OF NATURAL HISTORY

15 Freer Gallery of Art

11TH

12TH

E ST.

G ST.

F ST.

PENNSYLVANIA AVE.

NEW YORK AVE.

12TH

CASE MEMORIAL BRIDGE

13TH

I ST.

H ST.

17

MUS OF AMERICAN HISTORY

14TH

15TH

18

WASHINGTON MONUMENT

19

CHERRY TREES

20 JEFFERSON MEMORIAL

16TH Lafayette SQUARE

WHITE HOUSE

THE ELLIPSE Zero Milestone

CONSTITUTION AVE.

KUTZ MEMORIAL BRIDGE

TIDAL BASIN

21

DECATUR HOUSE

22

OFFICE BLDG.

RENWICK GALLERY

CORCORAN GALLERY

23

24

25 26

OCTAGON HOUSE

17TH

18TH

E ST.

PAN AMERICAN UNION

CONSTITUTION HALL

REFLECTING POOL

JAPANESE LANTERN

CHERRY TREES

INDEPENDENCE AVE.

27

19TH

20TH

21ST

22ND

23RD

24TH

25TH

26TH

PENNSYLVANIA AVE.

I ST.

H ST.

G ST.

NEW HAMPSHIRE AVE.

NATIONAL ACADEMY OF SCIENCES

29

28

30

LINCOLN MEMORIAL

31

C ST.

POTOMAC RIVER

ARLINGTON MEMORIAL BRIDGE

32 JOHN F. KENNEDY CENTER

THEODORE ROOSEVELT MEMORIAL BRIDGE

THEODORE ROOSEVELT MEMORIAL BRIDGE

18

MALL CULTURAL INSTITUTIONS—BY MAP NUMBER

MALL CULTURAL INSTITUTIONS—ALPHABETICAL

ARCHITECTURAL LANDMARKS (Continued)

Building	Architect	Date	Map Page
Jefferson Memorial	John Russell Pope	1943	18
Library of Congress	Smithmeyer & Pelz	1897	16
Lincoln Memorial	Henry Bacon	1922	18
Martin Luther King Library	Mies Van der Rohe	1972	68
National Air & Space Mus.	Gyo Obata	1976	18
Nat'l Gallery Art-East Wing	I. M. Pei	1978	18
Nat'l Gallery Art-West Wing	John Russell Pope	1941	18
National Geographic Society	Edward Durrell Stone	1964	76
Octagon House	Dr. William Thornton	1800	18
Old Pension Building	Gen. Montgomery Meigs	1883	16
Old Post Office	W. Edbrooke	1899	16
Pan American Health	Roman Fresnedo-Siri	1964	16
Pan American Union	Al Kelsey, Paul Cret	1910	16
Phillips Gallery	Hornblower, Marshall	1897	18
Portrait Gallery	Wm. Elliott R. Mills	1867	18
Pre-Columbian Museum	Philip Johnson	1963	76
Renwick Gallery	James Renwick	1859	18
Smithsonian	James Renwick	1849	18
Supreme Court	Cass Gilbert	1935	16
Treasury	R. Mills, T.V. Walter	1869	16
Washington Monument	Robert Mills	1885	18
White House	J. Hoban, Benjamin Latrobe	1792	16
Union Station	Daniel H. Burnham	1908	16
Vietnam Vets' Wall/Statue	Maya Ying Lin/Frank Hart	1984	18

Church	Date	Architect	Church	Date	Architect
All Souls Unitarn-1924		Coolidge/Shattuck	Metropolitan AME-1885		Samuel Morsell
Christ Church-1805		Benj H Latrobe	St John's-1816		Benjamin Latrobe
Friends Meetng House-1930		Walter Price	St Mary's Episc-1887		Renwick, Aspinwall
Holy Trinity Parish-1851		Francis Stanton	St Matthew's Cath.-1899		Heines/LaFarge
Luther Memorial-1870		Judson York	Washington Cath.-1907		Philip H Frohman

FOR CHURCH LOCATIONS PAGE 52

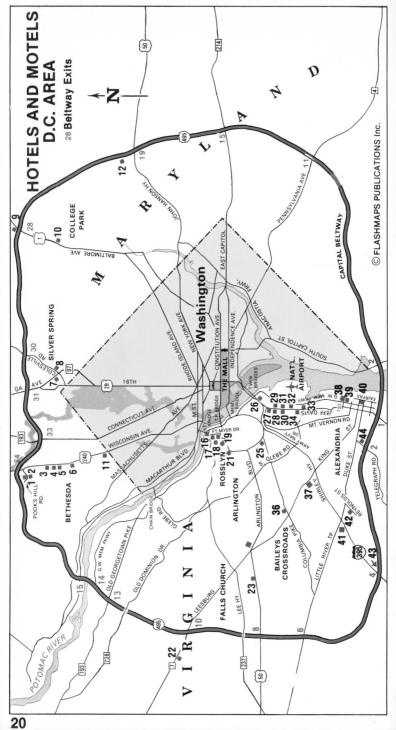

HOTELS AND MOTELS
D.C. AREA
28 Beltway Exits

N

© FLASHMAPS PUBLICATIONS Inc.

20

HOTELS & MOTELS DC AREA—BY MAP NUMBERS

1 Marriott	11 Holiday Chevy	26 Embassy Suites	36 Spring Hill
2 Linden Hill	12 Sheraton Hotel	26 Holiday Crowne	37 Radisson
3 Ramada Bthsd	16 Marriott Ky Br	28 Marriott Gate	38 Ramada Old
4 American Inn	17 BW Westpark	29 Holiday Arprt	39 BW Old Colny
5 Holiday Bthsd	18 Hyatt Key Brdg	30 Days Inn	40 Holiday Inn
6 Manor Inn	19 Holiday Key Brd	31 Marriott Crys	40 Morrison Hse
7 Holiday Silvr Sp	21 Quality Inn	31 Sheraton Crys	41 Days Inn
8 Sheraton Wash	22 Marriott-Tysons	32 Stouffers	42 Guest Qrters
9 Holiday Col Prk	23 Quality Gov	33 Hyatt Crystal	43 Hilton Inn
10 Quality Inn Coll	25 Sheraton Natl	34 Howard Johnsn	44 Holiday Teleg

HOTELS & MOTELS DC AREA

Hotel/Motel (Room Rate) ★	Address	Map No	Telephone	Rooms
American Inn (c)	8130 Wisconsin Ave, Bthesda	4	(301) 656-9300	72
BW Old Colony Inn (b)	N Washington & 1st Street	39	(703) 548-6300	223
BW Westpark (b)	1900 N Ft Meyer Dr, Rosslyn	17	(703) 527-4814	307
Days Inn (c)	I-395 & Rt 236, W Alexandria	41	(703) 354-4950	200
Days Inn Arlington (c)	2000 Jeff Davis Hwy, Arl	30	(703) 920-8600	250
Embassy Suites (a+)	1300 Jeff Davis Hwy, Arl	26	(703) 979-9799	267
Guest Quarters (a)	100 S Reynolds, Alexandria	42	(703) 370-9600	215
Hilton Inn Sprngfld (b+)	6550 Loisdale Road	43	(703) 971-8900	246
Holiday Crowne Plaza (a)	300 Army Navy Dr, Arlington	26	(703) 892-4100	635
Holiday Inn-Airport (b+)	1489 Jeff Davis Hwy, Arlngtn	29	(703) 521-1600	308
Holiday Inn-Bethesda (b)	8120 Wisconsin Ave, Bethsda	5	(301) 652-2000	267
Holiday Inn-Chvy Chs (b)	5520 Wisconsin Ave	11	(301) 656-1500	223
Holiday Inn-Coll Prk (b)	10,000 Baltimore, College Pk	9	(301) 345-6700	123
Holiday Inn-Key Brdg (b)	1850 N Ft Meyer Dr	19	(703) 522-0400	178
Holiday Inn-Old Town (a)	480 King St, Alexandria	40	(703) 549-6080	228
Holiday Inn-Silver Spr (c)	8777 Georgia Ave	7	(301) 589-0800	231
Holiday Inn-Telegraph (b)	2460 Eisenhower Ave, Alex	44	(703) 960-3400	260
Howard Johnson's (b+)	2650 Jeff Davis Hwy, Arl	34	(703) 684-7200	275
Hyatt Key Bridge (a+)	1325 Wilson Blvd	18	(703) 525-1234	303
Hyatt Reg Cryst Cty (a+)	2799 Jeff Davis Hwy, Arl	33	(703) 486-1234	693
Linden Hill Hotel (c)	Pooks Hill Rd, Bethesda	2	(301) 530-0300	300
Manor Inn (c)	7740 Wisconsin Ave, Bethsda	6	(301) 656-2100	73
Marriott Bethesda (a+)	5151 Pooks Hill Rd, Bethesda	1	(301) 897-9400	410
Marriott-Cryst Cty (a+)	1999 Jefferson Davis Hwy	31	(703) 521-5500	340
Marriott Gateway (a+)	1700 Jeff Davis Hwy, Arlngtn	28	(703) 920-3230	454
Marriott-Key Bridge (a+)	1401 Lee Hwy, Rosslyn	16	(703) 524-6400	558
Marriott-Tysn Crner (a+)	8028 Leesburg Pike	22	(703) 734-3200	393
Morrison House (a+)	116 S Alfred, Alex (Old Town)	40	(703) 838-8000	47
Quality Inn-Arlington (b)	Arlington Blvd & Courthse, Arl	21	(703) 524-4000	400
Quality Inn-College Pk (c)	7200 Baltimore Ave	10	(301) 864-5820	175
Quality Inn-Governor (c)	6650 Arlington Blvd, Falls Ch	23	(703) 532-8900	123
Radisson Mark Plz (a+)	5000 Seminary Rd, Alex	37	(703) 845-1010	428
Ramada Inn-Bethesda (a)	8400 Wisconsin Ave	3	(301) 654-1000	163
Ramada Inn-Old Town (a)	901 N Fairfax, Alexandria	38	(703) 683-6000	255
Sheraton Crystal (a)	1800 Jeff Davis Hwy, Arl	31	(703) 486-1111	219
Sheraton Hotel (b)	8500 Annapolis Rd, New Carrll	12	(301) 459-6700	250
Sheraton National (a)	Columbia Pk & Wash Blvd, Arl	25	(703) 521-1900	431
Sheraton-Wash NW (b)	8727 Colesville Rd, Silver Spg	8	(301) 589-5200	283
Spring Hill Lodge (c)	5666 Columbia Pk, Bailys Crs	36	(703) 820-5600	60
Stouffers Cncourse (a+)	2399 Jeff Davis Hwy, Arl	32	(703) 979-6800	400

*ROOM RATES (DOUBLE): (a) $90-115   (b) $70-90   (c) $40-70   **21**

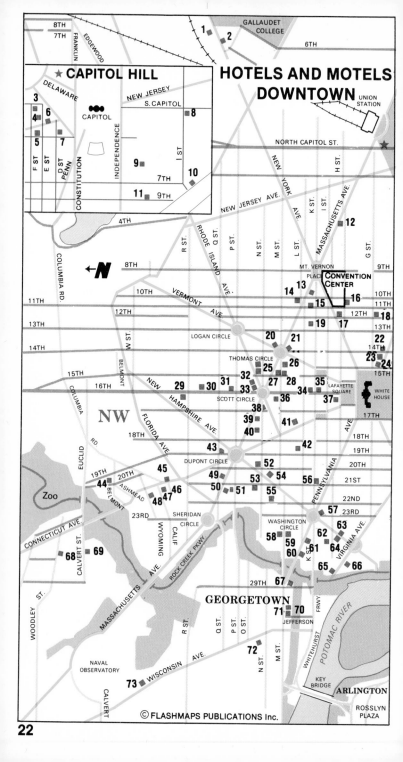

HOTELS AND MOTELS DOWNTOWN

★ **CAPITOL HILL**

DOWNTOWN HOTELS & MOTELS—BY MAP NUMBER

1 BW Regency	25 Ramada Inn Central	50 Ritz Carlton
2 Best West Envoy	26 Vista International	51 Georgetown Omni
3 Phoenix Park	27 Dolley Madison	52 Ramada Renaissnce
4 Bellevue Hotel	28 Madison Hotel	53 Hampshire Hotel
5 Sheraton Grand	29 Windsor Inn	54 Embassy Square
6 Quality Inn Capitol	30 Embassy Inn	55 Marriott Washington
7 Hyatt Regency	31 Quality Inn D'twn	56 Lombardy Hotel
8 Best West Skyline	32 Holiday Inn Central	57 One Washington Cir
9 Holiday Capitol	33 Radisson Park Terr	58 Park Hyatt
10 Channel Inn	34 Capital Hilton	59 Grand Hotel, The
11 Loew's L'Enfant Plz	35 Sheraton Carlton	59 Westin Washington
12 Comfort Inn	36 Jefferson Hotel	60 Guest Quarters
13 Henley Park	37 Hay-Adams Hotel	61 Bristol Wyndham
14 Harrington Hotel	38 Holiday Inn Gov	62 River Inn
15 Youth Hostel	39 Canterbury Hotel	63 Guest Quarters
16 Grand Hyatt	40 Tabard Inn	64 Inn Foggy Bottom
17 Holiday Crowne Plz	41 Mayflower Hotel	65 Howard Johnson
18 Morrison-Clark	42 Anthony Hotel	66 Watergate Hotel
19 Days Inn Conv Ctr	43 DuPont Plaza	67 Four Seasons
20 Washington Plaza	44 Rock Creek	68 Sheraton Washington
21 Holiday Inn Thos Cir	45 Washington Hilton	69 Shoreham Omni
22 Willard Intercontl	46 Highland Hotel	70 Georgetown Marbury
23 Marriott, J. W.	47 Quality Inn Conn	71 Georgetown Dutch
24 Washington Hotel	48 Normandy Inn	72 Georgetown Inn
25 General Scott	49 Embassy Row	73 Holiday-Georgetown

DOWNTOWN HOTELS & MOTELS

Hotel/Motel (Room Rate) ★	Address	Map No.	Telephone	Rooms
Anthony Hotel (b)	1823 L Street NW	42	223-4320	100
Bellevue Hotel (b)	15 E Street NW	4	638-0900	140
Best Western Envoy (c)	501 New York Ave NE	2	543-7400	73
BW Regency Congress (c)	600 New York Ave NE	1	546-9200	50
BW Skyline Inn (c)	10 Eye Street SW	8	488-7500	203
Bristol Wyndham (a)	2430 Penn Ave NW	61	955-6400	240
Canterbury, The (a)	1733 N Street NW	39	393-3000	99
Capital Hilton (a)	16th & K Street NW	34	393-1000	534
Channel Inn (b)	650 Water Street SW	10	554-2400	100
Comfort Inn (c)	500 H Street NW	12	289-5959	195
Days Inn Convention Ctr (c+)	12th & K Street, NW	19	842-1020	218
Dolley Madison, The (a)	1507 M Street NW	27	862-1876	42
DuPont Plaza (b)	DuPont Circle	43	483-6000	312
Embassy Inn (c)	1627 16th Street NW	30	234-7800	41
Embassy Row (a)	2015 Mass Ave NW	49	265-1600	194
Embassy Square (b)	2000 N Street, NW	54	659-9000	250
Four Seasons (a+)	2800 Penn Ave NW	67	342-0444	198
General Scott Inn (c)	1464 Rhode Island Ave	25	333-6700	65
Georgetown Dutch Inn (b)	1075 Thos Jefferson NW	71	337-0900	54
Georgetown Inn (a)	1310 Wisconsin NW	72	333-8900	95
Georgetown Marbury (b)	3000 M Street NW	70	726-5000	164
Georgetown Omni (a)	2121 P Street NW	51	293-3100	300
Grand Hotel, The (a)	2350 M Street NW	59	429-0100	263
Grand Hyatt (a+)	1000 H Street NW	16	582-1234	910
Guest-Quarters (b+)	801 New Hampshire NW	63	785-2000	101
Guest-Quarters (b+)	2500 Penn Ave NW	60	333-8060	123
Hampshire Hotel (b)	1310 New Hampshire	53	296-7600	82
Harrington Hotel (c)	11th & E Street NW	14	628-8140	300
Hay-Adams (a+)	800 16th Street NW	37	638-6600	165
Henley Park (a)	926 Mass Ave NW	13	638-5200	98

*ROOM RATES (DOUBLE): (a) $160-190 (b) $90-160 (c) $60-85 **23**

DOWNTOWN HOTELS & MOTELS Continued

Hotel/Motel (Room Rate) ★	Address	Map No.	Telephone	Rooms
Highland Hotel (b)	1914 Conn Ave NW	46	797-2000	140
Holiday-Capitol (b)	550 C Street SW	9	479-4000	529
Holiday Inn-Central (c)	1501 Rhode Island NW	32	483-2000	214
Holiday Inn-Georgetown (c)	2101 Wisconsin NW	73	338-4600	147
Holiday Inn-Governor's (b)	1615 Rhode Island NW	38	296-2100	161
Holiday Inn-Thomas Cir (c)	Mass & Thomas Circle	21	737-1200	207
Howard Johnson (b)	2601 Virginia NW	65	965-2700	190
Hyatt Regency (a)	400 New Jersey NW	7	737-1234	842
Inn at Foggy Bottom (b)	824 New Hampshire	64	337-6620	96
Jefferson Hotel (a)	16th Street & M NW	36	347-2200	104
Loew's L'Enfant Plaza (a)	480 l'Enfant Plaza SW	11	484-1000	373
Lombardy Hotel (b)	2019 Eye Street NW	56	828-2600	122
Madison Hotel (a+)	15th Street & M NW	28	862-1600	362
Marriott Washington (a)	1221 22nd Street NW	55	872-1500	350
Marriott, J. W. (a+)	1331 Penn Ave NW	23	393-2000	774
Mayflower Hotel (a+)	1127 Conn Ave NW	41	347-3000	720
Morrison-Clark Inn (b)	Massachusetts & L St	18	898-1200	54
Normandy Inn (c)	2118 Wyoming NW	48	483-1350	77
One Washington Circle (a)	1 Washington Circle NW	57	872-1680	150
Park Hyatt (a)	1201 24th Street NW	58	789-1234	233
Phoenix Park (a)	520 N Capitol NW	3	638-6900	87
Quality Inn-Capitol (b)	415 New Jersey NW	6	638-1616	350
Quality Inn-Conn Ave (c)	1900 Conn Ave NW	47	332-9300	145
Quality Inn Downtown (b)	1315 16th Street NW	31	232-8000	135
Radisson Park Terrace I (b)	1515 Rhode Island NW	33	232-7000	189
Ramada Inn Central (b)	1430 Rhode Island	25	462-7777	186
Ramada Renaissance (b)	1143 New Hampshire	52	775-0800	360
Ritz Carlton (a+)	2100 Mass Ave NW	50	835-2100	260
River Inn Hotel (b)	924 25th Street NW	62	337-7600	128
Rock Creek (c)	1925 Belmont NW	44	462-6007	52
Sheraton-Carlton (a+)	16th Street & K NW	35	638-2626	218
Sheraton Grand (a)	New Jersey Ave & F St	5	628-2100	265
Sheraton-Washington (b)	2660 Woodley NW	68	328-2000	1505
Shoreham Hotel Omni (a)	2500 Calvert NW	69	234-0700	800
Tabard Inn (c)	1739 N Street NW	40	785-1277	40
Vista International (a)	1400 M Street NW	26	429-1700	413
Washington Hilton (b)	1919 Conn Ave NW	45	483-3000	1150
Washington Hotel (b)	15th St & Penn Ave NW	24	638-5900	350
Washington Plaza (b)	Mass & Thomas Circle	20	842-1300	343
Watergate Hotel (a+)	2650 Virginia Ave NW	66	965-2300	238
Westin Washington DC (a+)	M Street & 24th NW	59	429-2400	400
Willard Intercontinental (a+)	1401 Penn Ave	22	628-9100	390
Windsor Inn (c)	1842 16th Street NW	29	667-0300	47
Youth Hostel (c)	1009 11th Street NW	15	737-2333	125

*ROOM RATES (DOUBLE): (a) $160-190   (b) $90-160   (c) $60-85
WASHINGTON DC HOTEL RESERVATIONS 289-2220 (800) 554-2220

CAPITOL HILL & WATER FRONT RESTAURANTS
BY MAP NUMBERS — Map page 25

1 Hawk & Dove	8 Monocle	15 Jonah's Oyster
2 Toscanni	9 Hunan's	16 Market Inn
3 Taverna Greek	10 Anton's	17 Apple of Eve
4 Jenkin's	11 Bullfeathers	18 Phillip's Flgshp
4 Stevan's	12 Powerscourt	19 Hogate's
5 Adirondacks	13 La Colline	20 700 Water St
6 Cafe Capri	14 Kelly's Irish Times	21 Pier 7
7 La Brasserie	15 Hugo's	22 Gangplank

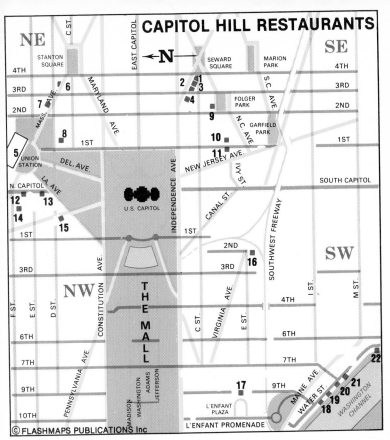

CAPITOL HILL RESTAURANTS

RESTAURANTS	Address	Map No	Cuisine	Price ★	Telephone
Adirondacks	Union Station	5	Amer Classic	$50 +	682-1840
Anton's Loyal Oppos	400 1st Street SE	10	American	20-25	546-4545
Apple of Eve	480 L'Enfant Plaza	17	Continental	35 +	484-1000
Bullfeathers	410 1st Street	11	American	25-30	543-5005
Cafe Capri	301 Mass Ave NE	6	Italian	17-20	546-5900
Gangplank	600 Water St SW	22	Seafood	20-25	554-5000
Hawk & Dove	329 Penn SE	1	American	12-15	543-3300
Hogate's	9th St & Maine SW	19	Seafood	20-25	484-6300
Hugo's	400 New Jersey NW	15	Steak/Sfd	40-45	737-1234
Hunan Capitol Hill	201 D St NE	9	Hunan/Szech	12-15	544-0102
Jenkin's Hill	223 Penn SE	4	American	12-15	544-6600
Jonah's Oyster	400 New Jersey NW	15	Seafood	20-25	737-1234
Kelly's Irish Times	14 F St NW	14	American	11-15	543-5433
La Brasserie	239 Mass NE	7	French	20-25	546-9154
La Colline	400 N Capitol NW	13	French	25-35	737-0400
Market Inn	200 E St SW	16	Seafood	15-20	554-2100
Monocle	107 D St NE	8	American	18-25	546-4488
Phillip's Flagship	900 Water St SW	18	Seafood	15-25	488-8515
Pier 7	650 Water St SW	21	Seafood/Stk	20-25	554-2500
Powerscourt, The	520 N Capitol NW	12	Irish Contl	25-35	737-3776
700 Water Street	700 Water St SW	20	American	15-20	554-7320
Stevan's on Hill	231 Penn SE	4	American	12-15	543-8337
Taverna Greek Isles	307 Penn SE	3	Greek	10-15	547-8360
Toscanini's	313 Penn SE	2	Italian	12-18	544-2338

★ *Prices do not include drinks or gratuities*

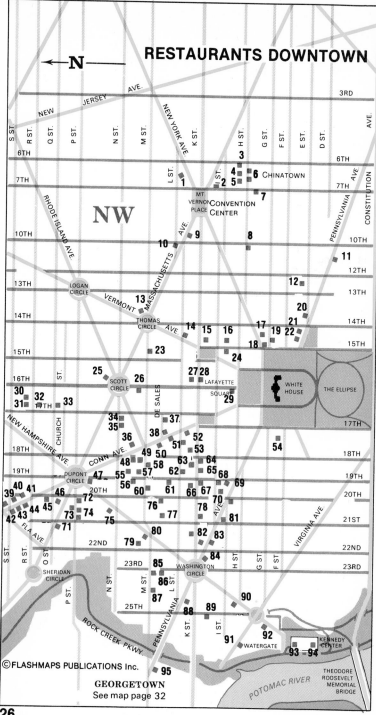

RESTAURANTS DOWNTOWN

← N

NW

Chinatown

MT. VERNON PLACE Convention Center

LOGAN CIRCLE

VERMONT

THOMAS CIRCLE

SCOTT CIRCLE

LAFAYETTE SQUARE

WHITE HOUSE

THE ELLIPSE

DE SALES

DUPONT CIRCLE

NEW HAMPSHIRE AVE.

CHURCH ST.

CONN. AVE.

FLA AVE.

SHERIDAN CIRCLE

WASHINGTON CIRCLE

VIRGINA AVE.

ROCK CREEK PKWY.

PENNSYLVANIA

WATERGATE

KENNEDY CENTER

THEODORE ROOSEVELT MEMORIAL BRIDGE

POTOMAC RIVER

© FLASHMAPS PUBLICATIONS Inc.

GEORGETOWN
See map page 32

26

DOWNTOWN RESTAURANTS — BY MAP NUMBERS

1 A. V. Ristorante	33 Boss Shepherds	64 Cafe Marche
2 Szechuan	34 Chaucer's	65 Shezan
3 Ruby	35 Iron Gate Inn	66 Tiberio
4 Tony Cheng's	36 Joe & Mo's	67 House of Hunan
5 China Inn	37 Nicholas	68 Charlie Chiang's
6 Big Wong	38 Charlie's Crab	69 Dominique's
6 Hunan's Chinatown	39 Ruth Chris	70 Devon Bar & Grill
7 Golden Palace	40 Anna Maria's	70 La Maree
8 Hamilton Chop Hse	41 Fourways	71 Jockey Club
9 Coeur de Lion	42 Katmandu	72 Nanking
10 Morrison-Clark	43 Cafe Petitto	73 Obelisk
11 Blossoms	43 Food for Thought	74 Galileo
11 Fitch Fox	43 Tokyo Sukiyaki	74 Bootsie, Winky
11 Hunan Pavilion	44 Odeon	75 Lafitte
12 Dankers	45 Childe Harold	76 Marrocco's
13 American Harvest	45 Vincenzo's	77 Il Giardino
14 Lenny's	46 Ambassador Grill	78 Prime Rib
15 Jacques	47 Front Page	79 Blackie's House
16 Peking	48 Cantina d'Italia	80 Giorgio's Tartufo
17 Old Ebbitt Grill	49 Astor	81 Primi Piatti
18 Prime Plus	50 Le Lion d'Or	82 Mr. K's
19 Skyroom	51 Mel Krupin's	82 Le Gaulois
20 Celadon	51 Twenty-One Federal	83 Trieste
21 Willard Room	52 Duke Ziebert's	84 West End Cafe
22 Occidental	52 Le Pavilion	85 Le Jardin
23 Montpelier Room	53 Harvey's	86 Mayfair, The
24 McPherson Grill	54 Maison Blanche	87 Colonnade, The
25 Chardonnay	55 Palm, The	88 Bristol Grill
26 Hunt Club	56 I Ricchi	89 Foggy Bottom
27 Trader Vic	56 Sichuan Garden	90 Gloria's
27 Twig's	57 Gusti's	91 Jean-Louis
28 Allegro	58 Gary's	91 Brighton Grill
29 John Hay Room	60 Jacqueline's	92 Les Champs
30 El Bodegon	61 Luigi's	93 Roof Terrace
31 La Fonda	62 Jean Pierre	94 Curtain Call
32 Annie's	63 Bombay Palace	95 Aux Beaux Champs

DOWNTOWN RESTAURANTS

Restaurant	Address	Map No.	Cuisine	Avg Dinner Price ★	Telephone
Allegro	Sheraton Carlton Hotl	28	Continental	$45 +	638-2626
Ambassador Grill	2015 Mass NW	46	Continental	25-35	265-1600
American Harvest	Vista Internatl Hotel	13	American	35-40	429-1700
Anna Maria's	1737 Conn NW	40	Italian	15-20	667-1444
Annie's Paramount	1609 17th St NW	32	Steak/Sfd	15-25	232-0395
Astor	1813 M St NW	49	Greek	10-14	331-7994
Aux Beaux Champs	2800 Penn Ave NW	95	French	45 +	342-0810
A.V. Ristorante	607 New York NW	1	Italian	14-20	737-0550
Big Wong	610 H St NW	6	Chinese	10-15	638-0116
Blackie's Hse of Beef	22nd St & M NW	79	American	17-24	333-1100
Blossoms	Old PO Pavilion	11	American	12-20	371-1838
Bombay Palace	1835 K St NW	63	No. Indian	12-15	331-0111
Bootsie Winky Maud	2026 P St NW	74	American	10-20	887-0900
Boss Shepherds	1527 17th St NW	33	Ital/Amer	12-16	328-8193
Brighton Grill	Watergate Hotel	91	Amer Contl	45-55	298-4455
Bristol Grill	Bristol Hotel	88	American	45 +	955-6400

★ Prices do not include drinks or gratuities

Restaurant	Address	Map No.	Cuisine	Avg Dinner Price ★	Telephone
Cafe Marche	1810 K St NW	64	French	$12-15	293-3000
Cafe Petitto	1724 Conn NW	43	Italian	12-15	462-8771
Cantina d'Italia	1214A 18th St NW	48	No. Italian	50-60	659-1830
Celadon	J W Marriott Hotel	20	Fr/Oriental	35-45	393-2000
Chardonnay	Park Terrace Hotel	25	New Amer	25-30	232-7000
Charlie Chiang's	1912 Eye St NW	68	Chinese	10-20	293-6000
Charlie's Crab	1101 Conn NW	38	Seafood	20-30	785-4505
Chaucer's	Canterbury Hotel	34	Continental	20-30	296-0665
Childe Harold	1610 20th St NW	45	American	15-20	483-6702
China Inn	631 H St NW	5	Chinese	10-20	842-0909
Coeur de Lion	Henley Pk Hotel	9	French	45 +	638-5200
Colonnade, The	Westin Washington	87	Continental	45-50	429-2400
Curtain Call Cafe	Kennedy Center	94	American	15-18	833-8870
Dankers	1209 E St NW	12	American	10-15	628-2330
Devon Bar & Grill	2000 Penn NW	70	Seafood	25-30	833-5660
Dominique's	1900 Penn NW	69	French	35-45	452-1126
Duke Ziebert's	1050 Conn NW	52	Steak/Sfd	25-35	466-3730
El Bodegon	1637 R St NW	30	Spanish	18-20	667-1710
Fitch, Fox, & Brown	Old PO Pavilion	11	Cont Amer	15-20	289-1100
Foggy Bottom Cafe	River Inn Hotel	89	American	12-18	338-8707
Food For Thought	1738 Conn NW	43	Vegetarian	9-12	797-1095
Fourways	1701 20th St NW	41	French	55 +	483-3200
Front Page	1333 New Hampshire	47	American	15-20	296-6500
Galileo	2014 P St NW	74	Italian	30-35	293-7191
Gary's	1800 M St NW	58	American	45 +	463-6470
Giorgio's Tartufo	1200 New Hampshire	80	No. Italian	35-45	293-0222
Gloria's	824 New Hamphire	90	No. Italian	18-22	333-2266
Golden Palace	720 7th St NW	7	Cantonese	10-18	783-1225
Gusti's	1837 M St NW	57	Italian	10-15	331-9444
Hamilton Chop Hse	Grand Hyatt Hotel	8	Steak/Sfd	40-50	582-1234
Harvey's	1001 18th St NW	53	Seafood	25-30	833-1858
House of Hunan	1900 K St NW	67	Chinese	12-20	293-9111
Hunans Chinatown	624 H St NW	6	Hunan/Szch	25-30	783-5858
Hunan at Pavilion	Old PO Pavilion	11	Chinese	12-14	371-2828
Hunt Club	Jefferson Hotel	26	European	35-45	467-4849
I Ricchi	1220 19th St NW	56	Tuscan	30-40	835-0459
Il Giardino	1110 21st St NW	77	Italian	45 +	223-4555
Iron Gate Inn	1734 N St NW	35	Mid East	15-20	737-1370
Jacqueline's	1990 M St NW	60	French	35-45	785-8877
Jacques	915 15th St NW	15	French	25-35	737-4445
Jean-Louis	Watergate Hotel	91	French	70 +	298-4488
Jean-Pierre	1835 K St NW	62	French	45 +	466-2022
Jockey Club	Ritz Carlton Htl	71	Fr Continl	45 +	659-8000
Joe & Mo's	1211 Conn NW	36	Steak	45 +	659-1211
John Hay Room	Hay Adams Hotel	29	French	40-45	638-6600
Katmandu	1800B Conn Ave	42	Nepali	18-24	483-6470
La Fonda	1639 R St NW	31	Mexican	15-20	232-6965
La Maree	1919 Eye St	70	French	45 +	659-4447
Lafitte	1310 New Hampshire	75	Fr Creole	14-20	296-7600
Le Gaulois	2133 Penn NW	82	French	20-30	466-3232
Le Jardin	1113 23rd St NW	85	French	12-15	457-0057
Le Lion d'Or	1150 Conn NW	50	French	55 +	296-7972
Le Pavillon	1050 Conn NW	52	Fr Nouvelle	50 +	833-3846
Lenny's	1025 Vermont NW	14	Continental	15-20	638-1313
Les Champs	600 New Hampshire	92	Continental	18-24	338-0700
Luigi's	1132 19th St NW	61	Italian	10-14	331-7574

★ Prices do not include drinks or gratuities

Restaurant	Address	Map No.	Cuisine	Avg Dinner Price ★	Telephone
Maison Blanche	1725 F St NW	54	French	$45 +	842-0070
Marrocco's	1120 20th St NW	76	Italian	12-20	331-9664
Mayfair, The	The Grand Hotel	86	Continental	50 +	955-4488
McPherson Grill	950 15th St NW	24	American	25-30	638-0950
Mel Krupin's	1120 Conn NW	51	American	45 +	331-7000
Montpelier Room	Madison Hotel	23	Fr Contl	45 +	862-1712
Morrison-Clark Inn	Mass Ave & L St	10	American	20-25	898-1200
Mr. K's	2121 K St NW	82	Chinese	40-50	331-8868
Nanking	2002 P St NW	72	Chinese	8-10	785-2208
Nicholas	Mayflower Hotel	37	American	25-35	347-8900
Obelisk	2029 P St NW	73	Regionl Ital	30.00	872-1180
Occidental	1475 Penn NW	22	Regionl Amer	45 +	639-8718
Odeon	1714 Conn NW	44	Italian	15-20	328-6228
Old Ebbitt Grille	675 15th St NW	17	American	25-35	347-4800
Palm, The	1225 19th St NW	55	American	45 +	293-9091
Peking	823 15th St NW	16	Chinese	9-12	737-4540
Prime Plus	727 15th St NW	18	Nouvlle Amer	45 +	783-0166
Prime Rib	2020 K St NW	78	American	45 +	466-8811
Primi Piatti	2013 Eye St NW	81	Italian	17-25	223-3600
Roof Terrace	Kennedy Center	93	Regionl Amer	25-30	833-8870
Ruby	609 H St NW	3	Chinese	9-12	842-0060
Ruth's Chris Stkhse	1801 Conn Ave NW	39	Steak	25-35	797-0033
Shezan	913 19th St NW	65	Pakistan	20-25	659-5555
Sichuan Garden	1220 19th St NW	56	Sichuan	19-25	296-4550
Skyroom	Hotel Washington	19	Fr Contl	30-35	638-5900
Szechuan	615 Eye St NW	2	Chinese	20-25	393-0130
Tiberio	1915 K St NW	66	Italian	65 +	452-1915
Tokyo Sukiyaki	1736 Conn NW	43	Japanese	12-17	462-7891
Tony Cheng's	619 H St NW	4	Mongolian	12-14	842-8669
Trader Vic's	Capital Hilton Hotel	27	Seafood	35-45	347-7100
Trieste	2138½ Penn NW	83	Italian	12-14	338-8444
Twenty-One Federal	1736 L St NW	51	Modrn Amer	60-70	331-9771
Twigs	Capital Hilton Hotel	27	American	25-35	393-1000
Vincenzo's	1606 20th St NW	45	Seafood	45 +	667-0047
West End Cafe	1 Wash Circle Hotel	84	Nouvelle	25-30	293-5390
Willard Room	Willard Hotel	21	American	45 +	628-9100

★ Prices do not include drinks or gratuities

OTHER DINING IN D.C. AND AREA

DINNER THEATERS	Address	Telephone
Burn Brae	Rte 29 Black Burn Rd, Burtonsville, Md	(301) 384-5800
Colony 7	Rte 32 & Baltimore/Washington Pkwy	(301) 953-2370
dc Space	7th Street & E, Washington DC	(202) 347-4960
Harlequin	1330 Gude Dr, Rockville, Md	(301) 340-8515
Hayloft	10501 Balls Ford Rd, Manassas, Va	(703) 631-0230
Lazy Susan Inn	Woodbridge, Virginia	(703) 550-7384
Little Theater	600 Wolfe Street, Alexandria, VA	(703) 683-0496
Petrucci's Main St	312 Main St, Laurel, Md	(301) 725-5226
Round House Thea	12210 Bushey Dr, Silver Spring, MD	(301) 468-4234
Toby's Dinner Thea	Route 29, Columbia, Md	(301) 730-8311
West End Dinner	4615 Duke St, Alex, Va	(703) 370-2500

POTOMAC CRUISE DINING

Potomac River Cruises	Zero Prince Street, Alexandria, Va	(703) 683-6076
Spirit of Washington	Pier 4, 6th & Water Street SW, DC	(202) 554-8000

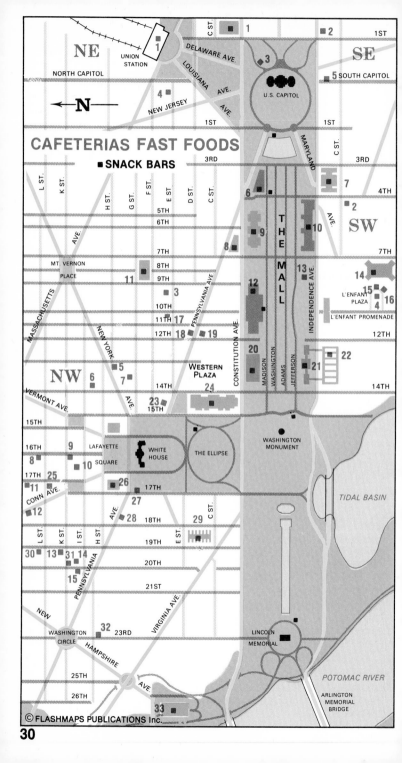

CAFETERIAS FAST FOODS
■ SNACK BARS

NE
UNION STATION
NORTH CAPITOL
←N

SE
U.S. CAPITOL
SOUTH CAPITOL

DELAWARE AVE.
LOUISIANA AVE.
NEW JERSEY AVE.
MARYLAND AVE.

1ST
C ST.
1ST
3RD
C ST.
3RD
4TH

THE MALL

SW

INDEPENDENCE AVE.

L'ENFANT PLAZA
L'ENFANT PROMENADE

NW
MT. VERNON PLACE
LAFAYETTE SQUARE
WHITE HOUSE
THE ELLIPSE
WESTERN PLAZA

WASHINGTON MONUMENT

TIDAL BASIN

MASSACHUSETTS AVE.
NEW YORK AVE.
VERMONT AVE.
CONNECTICUT AVE.
PENNSYLVANIA AVE.
CONSTITUTION AVE.
MADISON
WASHINGTON
ADAMS
JEFFERSON

L ST.
K ST.
H ST.
G ST.
F ST.
E ST.
D ST.
C ST.
5TH
6TH
7TH
8TH
9TH
10TH
11TH
12TH
14TH
15TH
16TH
17TH
18TH
19TH
20TH
21ST
23RD
25TH
26TH

I ST.
L ST.
K ST.
H ST.

NEW HAMPSHIRE AVE.
WASHINGTON CIRCLE
VIRGINIA AVE.

LINCOLN MEMORIAL

POTOMAC RIVER

ARLINGTON MEMORIAL BRIDGE

© FLASHMAPS PUBLICATIONS Inc.

30

CAFETERIAS/CAFES — BY MAP NUMBERS

1 New Senate Office	12 Mus Natural History	23 The Shops
2 Library Congress	13 Hirshhorn Cafe	24 Dept Commerce
3 Supreme Court	14 Dept Housing	25 Dutch Treat
4 Bellevue Hotel	15 Greenhouse	23 New Executive
5 Rayburn House Bldg	16 Gourmet Too	27 Executive Office
6 Natl Gallery Art New	17 Kitcheteria	28 Hot Shoppes
7 Dept Health Hum Res	18 Via Cucina Caffe	29 Dept Interior
8 Fed Trade Comm.	19 Pavilion-Old PO	30 Dutch Treat Two
9 Natl Gallery Art	20 Mus Amer History	31 China Gr/Sholl's
10 Air & Space	21 Dept Agriculture N	32 Garden Eat'n
11 National Portrait	22 Dept Agriculture S	33 Encore

CAFETERIAS & CAFES

Cafeteria/Cafe	Address	Map No	Hours
Air & Space Museum	7th & Independence	10	10:00-5:00
Bellevue Hotel	15 E St NW	4	7:00-8:00
China Grove	1990 K St NW	31	11:00-4:00
Dept of Agriculture-North	14th St & Independence	21	7:00-3:30
Dept of Agriculture-South	14th St & Independence	22	7:00-3:30
Dept of Commerce	14th St & Constitution	24	9:00-2:00
Dept Health Human Resources	330 Independence SW	7	7:00-3:00
Department of Housing	451 7th St SW	14	7:00-2:00
Dept of Interior	18th St & C NW	29	7:00-3:15
Dutch Treat	1710 L St NW	25	7:30-5:30
Dutch Treat Two	1901 L St NW	30	7:30-4:00
Encore Cafeteria	Kennedy Center	33	11:30-8:00
Executive Office Bldg	Pennsylvania Ave & 17th St	27	7:15-2:30
Federal Trade Commission	6th St & Pennsylvania NW	8	7:30-2:00
Garden of Eat'n	GWU 2300 H St NW	32	11:00-6:00
Gourmet Too	609 l'Enfant Plaza	16	6:00-5:30
Greenhouse, The Cafe	480 l'Enfant Plaza	15	6:30-5:00
Hirshhorn Outdoor Cafe	7th & Independence SW	13	May-Oct
Hot Shoppess	1750 Pennsylvania Ave NW	28	7:30-7:30
Kitcheteria	11th St & E NW	17	7:00-9:00
Library Congress Madison Bldg	101 Independence Ave	2	11:00-2:00
Museum of American History	12th & Constitution	20	11:00-8:00
Museum of Natural History	10th & Constitution	12	11:00-4:30
National Portrait Gallery	8th & 9th Sts NW	11	10:00-4:30
National Gallery of Art	6th & Constitution	9	10:00-4:00
National Gallery (New Wing)	4th & Constitution	6	11:00-4:00
New Executive Office Bldg	17th St & H NW	26	7:30-2:30
New Senate Office Dirksen	1st St & Constitution	1	7:30-3:30
Rayburn House Building	Independence Ave & 1st St	5	7:30-2:30
Sholl's-Colonial	1990 K St NW	31	7:00-8:00
Supreme Court Cafeteria	1 First St NE	3	7:30-2:00
Via Cucina Caffe	1001 Pennsylvania Ave	18	7:00-7:00
The Pavilion · Old Post Office	1100 Pennsylvania Ave NW	19	10:00-9:30

CATSKILLS DELI, ENRICO'S, FRENCH FRYE, FLYING FRUIT, INDIAN DELIGHT, INTERNATIONAL DOGS, PANDA CAFE, PEDESTRIAN CAFE, PEGASUS, TACO DON'S, TEXAS CATTLE, WINGMASTERS

The Shops	1331 Pennsylvania Ave	23	10:00-7:00

BAGEL PLACE, BOARDWALK FRIES, EVERYTHING YOGURT, HERBERT'S STUFT POTATOE, HOT COALS HUNAN EXPRESS, JERRY'S SUBS, JUNIPERO, KABUKI SUSHI, LE CAFE, PAPA'S CHICKEN, PRIMO'S DELI, ROY ROGERS, SLICE OF ITALY PIZZA, SONIA'S SWEETS, TERIYAKI & TEMPURA

FAST FOOD — BY MAP NUMBERS

1 Union Station	6 McDonald's	11 Lion's Market
2 Roy Rogers	7 Roy Rogers	12 McDonald's
3 Arby's	8 Blue Chip	13 McDonald's
4 Roy Rogers	9 Burger King	14 Wendy's
5 German Deli	10 Hardees	15 Roy Rogers

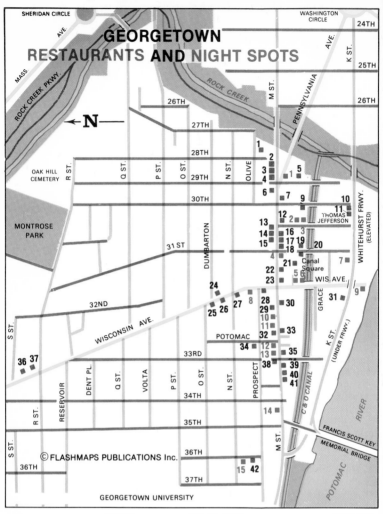

GEORGETOWN
RESTAURANTS AND NIGHT SPOTS

	Address	Map No.	Type	Telephone
Bayou, The	3135 K St NW	7	Rock/Dancing	333-2897
Blues Alley	1073 Wisconsin	5	Jazz/Blues	337-4141
Champions	1206 Wisconsin	8	DJ & Dancing	965-4005
Chelsea's	1055 Thos Jefferson	2	Live Bands/Performers	298-8222
dc Space	433 7th St NW	off	Cabaret/Music/Films	347-4960
Desiree	Four Seasons Hotel	1	Disco/Dancing	342-0820
F. Scott's	1232 36th NW	15	DJ & Dancing	965-1789
Flutes	1025 Thos Jefferson	3	DJ/Dancing	333-7333
J & B Crazy Horse	3259 M St NW	13	Live Rock	333-0400
Mr. Smith's	3104 M St NW	4	Jazz/Blues/Guitar	333-3104
Paul Mall	3235 M St NW	10	Rock/Dancing	965-5353
Poseur's	3403 M St NW	14	New Wave	965-5600
River Club	3233 K St NW	9	DJ/Band/Jazz/Blues	333-8118
Saloon, The	3239 M St	11	Live Jazz	338-4900
1063	1063 Wisconsin	6	Dancing	342-7373
Winston's	3295 M St NW	12	Disco	333-3150

32

GEORGETOWN RESTAURANTS — BY MAP NUMBERS

1	Hunan Garden	12	Leo Linda's	23	Nathan's	33	Clyde's
2	Caesar's	13	Charing Cross	24	Au Pied de	34	Morton's
3	Enriqueta's	14	Chez Grand	25	Sarinah	35	El Caribe
4	La Chaumiere	15	G'town Sfd	26	G'twn Grill	36	La Nicoise
5	Aux Beaux	16	Dar Es Salam	27	Martin's	37	Japan Inn
6	Guards, The	17	Le Steak	28	Third Edition	38	Las Pampas
7	Vietnam G'twn	18	Apana	29	Uno's	39	Tandoor
9	Foundry	19	Tout Va Bien	30	Houlihan's	40	Madurai
10	China Regency	20	Sea Catch	30	Samurai	41	Bamiyan
10	Tony's Joe	21	Cafe La Ruche	31	Chadwick's	42	1789, The
11	Hisago	22	Bistro Francais	32	Fettoosh		

GEORGETOWN RESTAURANTS

Restaurant	Address	Map No.	Cuisine	Average Price ★	Telephone
Apana	3066 M St NW	18	Indian	20-25	965-3040
Au Pied de Cochon	1335 Wisconsin	24	French	10-14	333-5440
Aux Beaux Champs	Four Seasons Hotel	5	French	45+	342-0810
Bamiyan	3320 M St NW	41	Afghan	20-25	338-1896
Bistro Francais	3128 M St NW	22	French	18-20	338-3830
Caesar's	2809 M St NW	2	Italian	15-20	337-0730
Cafe La Ruche	1039 31st St NW	21	French	12-15	965-2684
Chadwick's G'town	3205 K St NW	31	American	8-12	333-2565
Charing Cross	3027 M St NW	13	Italian	10-15	338-2141
Chez Grandmere	3057 M St NW	14	French	30-45	337-2436
China Regency	3000 K St NW	10	Szech/Hunan	16-20	944-4266
Clyde's	3236 M St NW	33	American	15-20	333-0294
Dar Es Salam	3056 M St NW	16	Moroccan	30-45	342-1925
El Caribe	3288 M St NW	35	Latin-Amer	25-35	338-3121
Enriqueta's	2811 M St NW	3	Mexican	20-25	338-7772
Fettoosh	3277 M St NW	32	Lebanese	12-18	342-1199
Foundry, The	1050 30th St NW	9	American	15-25	337-1500
G'town Bar & Grill	1310 Wisconsin	26	American	20-25	337-7777
G'town Seafood	3063 M St NW	15	Seafood	20-30	333-7038
Guards, The	2915 M St NW	6	American	20-30	965-2350
Hisago	3050 K St NW	11	Japanese	45-60	944-4282
Houlihan's	3222 M St NW	30	American	12-18	342-2280
Hunan Garden	1201 28th St NW	1	Szechuan	10-14	965-6800
Japan Inn	1715 Wisconsin	37	Japanese	20-30	337-3400
La Chaumiere	2813 M St NW	4	French	30-45	338-1784
La Nicoise	1721 Wisconsin	36	French	25-35	965-9300
Las Pampas	3291 M St NW	38	Argentinian	20-25	333-5151
Le Steak	3060 M St NW	17	Steak	20-25	965-1627
Leo 'n Linda's	1075 Thos Jefferson	12	American	20-25	333-0933
Madurai	3318 M St NW	40	Vegetarian	8-10	333-0997
Martin's Tavern	1264 Wisconsin	27	American	10-15	333-7370
Morton's of Chicago	3251 Prospect St	34	Beef/Lobster	45+	342-6258
Nathan's	3150 M St NW	23	No. Italian	30-35	338-2000
Samurai Japan Steak	3222 M St NW	30	Japanese	10-20	333-1001
Sarinah Satay	1338 Wisconsin	25	Indonesian	15-18	337-2955
Sea Catch	1054 31st St NW	20	Seafood	12-20	337-8855
1789, The	1226 36th St NW	42	American	45+	965-1789
Tandoor	3316 M St NW	39	Indian	18-25	333-3376
Third Edition	1218 Wisconsin	28	American	14-18	333-3700
Tony's & Joe	3000 K St NW	10	Seafood	20-30	944-4545
Tout Va Bien	1063 31 st St NW	19	French	25-30	965-1212
Uno's Chicago	3211 M St NW	29	Pizza	9-14	965-6333
Vietnam Georgetown	2934 M St NW	7	Vietnamese	12-16	337-4536

★ Prices do not include drinks or gratuities

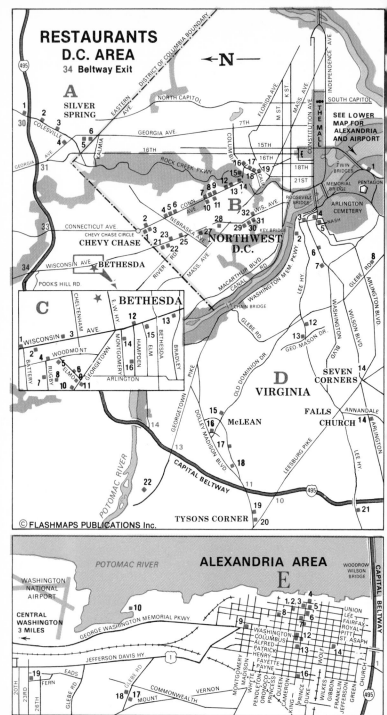

RESTAURANTS
D.C. AREA
34 Beltway Exit

← N →

A SILVER SPRING

B NORTHWEST D.C.

C BETHESDA

D VIRGINIA

SEE LOWER MAP FOR ALEXANDRIA AND AIRPORT

CHEVY CHASE CIRCLE
CHEVY CHASE
BETHESDA

SEVEN CORNERS

FALLS CHURCH

McLEAN

TYSONS CORNER

© FLASHMAPS PUBLICATIONS Inc.

ALEXANDRIA AREA

E

WASHINGTON NATIONAL AIRPORT

CENTRAL WASHINGTON 3 MILES ←

POTOMAC RIVER

WOODROW WILSON BRIDGE

CAPITAL BELTWAY

34

RESTAURANTS—D.C. AREA

SILVER SPRING A-Area

Restaurant	Address	Map No.	Cuisine	Average Price ★	(Area 301) Telephone
Crisfield's	8012 Georgia	A5	Seafood	$25-30	589-1306
Fred & Harry's	10110 Colesville	A1	Seafood	12-20	593-7177
Mamma Regina	8727 Colesville	A3	Italian	12-18	585-1040
Mrs. K's Tollhouse	9201 Colesville	A2	American	15-20	589-3500
Sakura Palace	7926 Georgia	A6	Japanese	15-25	587-7070
Wellington's	8777 Georgia	A4	Sfd/Beef	12-16	587-4600

NORTHWEST DC B-Area

(Area 202)

Restaurant	Address	Map No.	Cuisine	Average Price ★	Telephone
Adriatico	4515 Wisconsin	B27	Italian	12-17	686-1882
Austin Grill	2404 Wisconsin	B30	So. Western	12-16	337-8080
Cafe Burgundy	5031 Conn Ave	B4	French	12-16	686-5300
Caffe Italiano	3516 Conn Ave	B11	Italian	15-20	966-2172
Calvert Restaurant	1967 Calvert	B15	Mid-East	10-15	232-5431
Dancing Crab	4611 Wisconsin	B25	Seafood	12-18	244-1882
David Lee's Empress	1875 Conn Ave	B19	Chinese	10-15	462-8110
El Caribe	1828 Columbia	B17	Latin Amer	12-20	234-6969
Fishery, The	5511 Conn Ave	B2	Seafood	17-25	363-2144
Floriana	4936 Wisconsin	B22	No. Italian	17-23	362-9009
Germaine's	2400 Wisconsin	B31	Vietnamese	25-35	965-1185
Hunan Gallery	3308 Wisconsin	B28	Chinese	10-15	362-6645
Ivy's Place	3520 Conn Ave	B10	Thai/Indnsia	16-22	363-7802
La Fourchette	2429 18th St	B16	French	20-25	332-3077
L'Escargot	3309 Conn Ave	B9	French	14-20	966-7510
Le Caprice	2348 Wisconsin	B31	French	20-25	337-3394
Napoleon's	2649 Conn Ave	B13	French	15-20	265-8955
New Orleans Emprum	2477 18th St	B17	Cajun	15-20	328-3421
Old Europe	2434 Wisconsin	B29	German	15-20	333-7600
Omega	1858 Columbia	B18	Latin Amer	10-16	745-9158
Peking	5522 Conn Ave	B1	Chinese	10-12	966-8079
Petitto's	2653 Conn Ave	B12	Italian	20-25	667-5350
Pleasant Peasant	5300 Wisconsin	B21	American	20-25	364-2500
Red Sea	2463 18th St NW	B16	Ethiopian	8-14	483-5000
Roma	3419 Conn Ave	B8	Ital/Amer	12-16	363-6611
Round Table	4859 Wisconsin	B23	Ital/Sfd	10-16	362-1250
Shanghai Garden	4469 Conn Ave	B6	Chinese	9-13	362-3000
Sushi-Ko	2309 Wisconsin	B32	Japanese	20-25	333-4187
Swiss Cafe	5510 Conn Ave	B3	Continental	18-22	966-7600
Thai Room	5037 Conn Ave	B5	Thai	12-15	244-5933
Tucson Cantina	2605 Conn Ave	B14	Mexican	10-14	462-6410
Yenching Palace	3524 Conn Ave	B10	Chinese	10-15	362-8200

BETHESDA C-Area

(Area 301)

Restaurant	Address	Map No.	Cuisine	Average Price ★	Telephone
Bacchus-Bethesda	7945 Norfolk Ave	C8	Lebanese	17-22	657-1722
Benihana of Tokyo	7315 Wisconsin	C12	Japanese	15-25	652-5391
Bish Thompson's	7935 Wisconsin	C10	Seafood	15-20	656-2400
China Coral	6900 Wisconsin	C13	Chinese	12-14	656-1203
China Garden	4711 Montgomery	C14	Chinese	10-15	657-4665
Frascati	4806 Rugby	C7	Italian	15-20	652-9514
Joe's Fresh Sfd	4723 Elm St	C15	Amer/Sfd	12-20	654-1530
Kabul West	4918 Cordell Ave	C9	Afghan	16-20	986-8566
Kaori Hana	7944 Wisconsin	C3	Japanese	18-20	951-8771
La Luna	4846 Cordell Ave	C9	Sicilian	17-25	654-4600
Matuba-Bethesda	4918 Cordell Ave	C9	Japanese	12-20	652-7449
Michel's	7904 Woodmont	C5	French	12-17	656-7922
North China	7814 Old G'town	C11	Chinese	10-15	656-7922

★ *Prices do not include drinks or gratuities*

Restaurant	Address	Map No	Cuisine	Price ★	Telephone
O'Donnell's Sea Grill	8301 Wisconsin	C1	Seafood	$12-15	656-6200
Pines of Rome	4709 Hampden	C16	Italian	10-17	657-8775
Raleigh Inn	8011 Woodmont	C4	American	12-16	652-4244
Rendez-vous Cafe	8120 Wisconsin	C2	Varied	11-17	652-2000
Rio Grande	4919 Fairmont	C6	TexMex	16-19	656-2981
Vagabond	7315 Wisconsin	C12	Centrl Eurp	15-20	654-2575

VIRGINIA D-Area

(Area 703)

Restaurant	Address	Map No	Cuisine	Price	Telephone
Alpine	4770 Lee Hwy	D12	Italian	15-20	528-7600
Aspara	6769 Wilson Blvd	D14	Thai	15-20	241-0158
Bangkok Gourmet	523 S 23rd Arl	D3	Thai	24-30	521-1305
Casa Maria	Rte123-Tysons	D19	Mexican	10-15	893-2443
Charlie's Place	6930 Old Dom Dr	D15	American	15-20	893-1034
Company Inkwell	8240 Leesbrg Pike	D20	French	45+	356-0300
Da Domenico	1992 Chain Brdge	D18	No. Italian	35-40	790-9000
Evans Farm Inn	1696 Chain Brdge	D17	American	20-25	356-8000
Fuji	77 N Glebe	D8	Korean/Jap	12-17	524-3666
Hsian Foong	1836 Wilson Blvd	D6	Chinese	10-15	528-8886
Kazan's	6813 Redmond	D16	Mid-East	12-20	734-1960
La Guinguette	8111 Lee Hwy	D21	French	30-35	560-3220
L'Alouette	2045 Wilson Blvd	D7	French	15-20	525-1750
L'Auberge Chez Fran.	332 Springvale Rd	D22	French	25-30	759-3800
Orleans House	1213 Wilson Blvd	D3	American	10-15	524-2929
Penthouse	Holiday Crowne Plz	D1	Continental	35-45	892-4100
Queen Bee	3181 Wilson Blvd	D7	Vietnamese	7-12	527-3444
Shanghai	5157 Lee Hwy	D13	Chinese	9-14	536-7446
Stars	Sheraton National	D1	Contl/Amer	25-35	521-1900
Top o' the Town	14th & N Oak	D5	Continental	20-25	525-9200
View, The	Marriott-Key Brdge	D2	Continental	25-30	524-6400
Windows	1000 Wilson Blvd	D4	Amer Nvlle	30-35	527-4430

ALEXANDRIA & AIRPORT E-Area

(Area 703)

Restaurant	Address	Map No	Cuisine	Price	Telephone
Bamiyan II	300 King St	E7	Afghan	13-18	548-9006
Chez Andre	10 E Glebe St	E18	French	45+	836-1404
Chez Froggy	509 S 23rd St	E17	French	45+	979-7676
China Gate	310 N Fairfax	E8	Chinese	10-15	548-8080
Fish Market	105 King Street	E2	Seafood	15-25	836-5676
Gadsby's Tavern	138 N Royal St	E7	American	12-18	548-1288
Geno's	1300 King Street	E16	Ital/Amer	10-14	549-1796
Geranio	722 King Street	E12	Italian	25-35	548-0088
Henry Africa	607 King Street	E12	French	40-50	549-4010
Il Porto	121 King Street	E1	Italian	14-20	836-8833
Kristos Charcoal Hse	608 Montgomery	E9	Beef	12-15	683-9864
La Bergerie	218 N Lee Street	E1	French	35+	683-1007
Landini Brothers	115 King Street	E2	Ital/Seafd	15-25	836-8404
Le Chardon d'Or	116 S Alfred St	E13	Fr Nouvelle	45-65	838-8008
Le Refuge	127 N Washingtn	E12	French	20-25	548-4661
Portofino	526 S 23rd St	E19	Italian	25-35	979-8200
Potowmack Landing	Washington Marina	E10	Seafood	21-26	548-0001
Scotland Yard	728 King Street	E12	Scotch	20-25	683-1742
Seaport Inn, The	6 King Street	E4	Stk/Seafd	15-20	549-2341
Taverna Cretekou	818 King Street	E13	Greek	25-35	548-8688
Terrazza	710 King Street	E12	Italian	40-45	683-6900
Two-Nineteen	219 King Street	E7	Fr Creole	20-25	549-1141
Warehouse B&G	214 King Street	E6	Seafood	20-25	683-6868
Wayfarer	110 S Pitt Street	E6	English	15-25	836-2749
Wharf, The	119 King Street	E3	Seafood	20-30	836-2834

★ *Prices do not include drinks or gratuities*

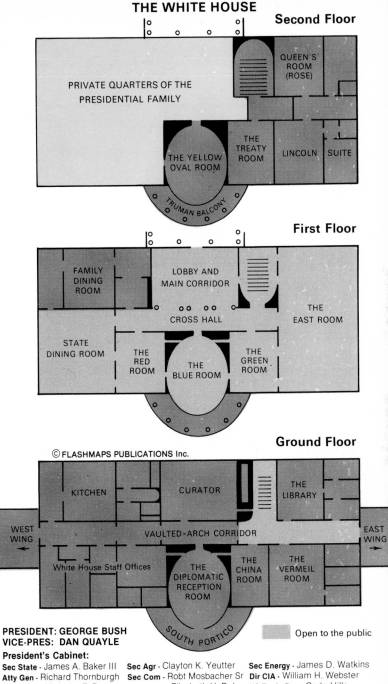

THE WHITE HOUSE

Second Floor
First Floor
Ground Floor

© FLASHMAPS PUBLICATIONS Inc.

Open to the public

PRESIDENT: GEORGE BUSH
VICE-PRES: DAN QUAYLE

President's Cabinet:

Sec State · James A. Baker III
Atty Gen · Richard Thornburgh
Sec Treas · Nicholas F. Brady
Sec Int · Manuel Lujan, Jr
Sec Ed · Lauro F. Cavazos
Sec Veterans · Edw Derwinski

Sec Agr · Clayton K. Yeutter
Sec Com · Robt Mosbacher Sr
Sec Labor · Elizabeth H. Dole
Sec Health · Louis W. Sullivan
Sec Housing · Jack F. Kemp
Sec Trans · Samuel K. Skinner

Sec Energy · James D. Watkins
Dir CIA · William H. Webster
US Trade Rep · Carla Hills
Mngm-Budgt · Richard Darman
UN Ambass · Thomas Pickering
Dir FBI · William Sessions

37

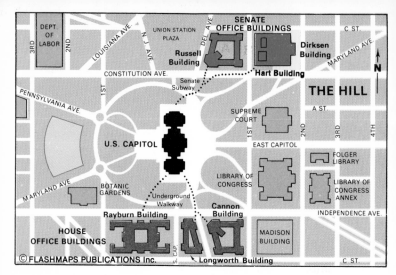

THE 101st CONGRESS

THE SENATE

Vice-President : Dan Quayle
Pres. Pro Temp : Robert C. Byrd
Majority Leader : George Mitchell
Majority Whip : Alan Cranston
Minority Leader : Robert Dole
Minority Whip : Alan K. Simpson

HOUSE OF REPRESENTATIVES

Speaker : Jim Wright
Majority Leader : Thomas S. Foley
Majority Whip : Tony Coelho
Minority Leader : Robert H. Michel
Minority Whip : Richard Cheney

SENATE AND HOUSE Terms end January 3rd
SENATE TERM : 6 Years   **HOUSE TERM : 2 Years**
Names in Blue   Names in Black

CONGRESSIONAL DIRECTORY—BY STATE
Congressional Telephone Number: (202) 224-3121

ALABAMA

Heflin, Howell (D)	Term - 1991
Shelby, Richard C. (D)	Term: 1993
Bevill, Tom (D)	4th District
Callahan, H. L. (R)	1st District
Dickinson, William (R)	2nd District
Erdreich, Ben (D)	6th District
Flippo, Ronnie G (D)	5th District
Harris, Claude (D)	7th District
Nichols, Bill (D)	3rd District

ALASKA

Murkowski, Frank (R)	Term - 1993
Stevens, Ted (R)	Term - 1991
Young, Donald E. (R)	At Large

ARIZONA

De Concini, Dennis (D)	Term - 1995
McCain, John (R)	Term - 1993
Kolbe, Jim (R)	5th District
Kyl, Jon (R)	4th District
Rhodes, John III (R)	1st District
Stump, Bob (D)	3rd District
Udall, Morris K (D)	2nd District

ARKANSAS

Bumpers, Dale (D)	Term - 1993
Pryor, David H (D)	Term - 1989
Alexander, Bill (D)	1st District
Anthony, Beryl, Jr. (D)	4th District
Hammerschmidt, J (R)	3rd District
Robinson, Tommy (D)	2nd District

CONGRESSIONAL DIRECTORY (Continued)

Congressional Telephone Number: (202) 224-3121

CALIFORNIA

Cranston, Alan (D)	Term - 1993
Wilson, Pete (R)	Term - 1995
Anderson, Glenn M. (D)	32nd District
Bates, Jim (D)	44th District
Beilenson, Anthony (D)	23rd District
Berman, Howard L (D)	26th District
Bosco, Douglas H. (D)	1st District
Boxer, Barbara (D)	6th District
Brown, George E. (D)	36th District
Campbell, Tom (R)	12th District
Coelho, Tony (D)	15th District
Cox, Christopher (R)	40th District
Dannemeyer, Wm (R)	39th District
Dellums, Ronald V. (D)	8th District
Dixon, Julian (D)	28th District
Dornan, Robert K (R)	38th District
Dreir, Dave (R)	33rd District
Dymally, Mervyn (D)	31st District
Edwards, Don (D)	10th District
Fazio, Vic (D)	4th District
Gallegly, Elton (R)	21st District
Hawkins, Augustus (D)	29th District
Herger, Wally (R)	2nd District
Hunter, Duncan (R)	45th District
Lagomarsino, Robt. (R)	19th District
Lantos, Tom (D)	11th District
Lehman, Richard (D)	18th District
Levine, Mel (D)	27th District
Lewis, Jerry (R)	35th District
Lowery, Bill (R)	41st District
Martinez, Matthew (D)	30th District
Matsui, Robert (D)	3rd District
McCandless, Al (R)	37th District
Miller, George (D)	7th District
Mineta, Norman (D)	13th District
Moorhead, Carlos (R)	22nd District
Packard, Ronald (R)	43rd District
Panetta, Leon (D)	16th District
Pashayan, Charles (R)	17th District
Pelosi, Nancy (D)	5th District
Rohrabacher, Dana (R)	42nd District
Roybal, Edward R. (D)	25th District
Shumway, Norman (R)	14th District
Stark, Fortney (D)	9th District
Thomas, William (R)	20th District
Torres, Esteban (D)	34th District
Waxman, Henry (D)	24th District

COLORADO

Armstrong, William (R)	Term - 1991
Wirth, Timothy E (D)	Term - 1993
Brown, Hank (R)	4th District
Hefley, Joel (R)	5th District
Campbell, Ben (D)	3rd District
Schaefer, D. L.(R)	6th District
Schroeder, Patricia (D)	1st District
Skaggs, David (D)	2nd District

CONNECTICUT

Dodd, Christopher J.	Term - 1993
Lieberman, Joe (D)	Term - 1995
Gejdenson, Sam (D)	2nd District
Johnson, Nancy L (R)	6th District
Kennelly, Barbara B (D)	1st District
Morrison, Bruce (D)	3rd District
Rowland, John G (R)	5th District
Shays, Christopher (R)	4th District

DELAWARE

Biden, Joseph Jr. (D)	Term - 1991
Roth, William V. Jr. (R)	Term - 1995
Carper, Thomas R (D)	At-Large

DISTRICT OF COLUMBIA

Fauntroy, Walter E (D)

FLORIDA

Chiles, Lawton (D)	Term - 1991
Graham, Bob (D)	Term - 1993
Bennett, Charles E. (D)	3rd District
Bilirakis, Michael (R)	9th District
Fascell, Dante B. (D)	19th District
Gibbons, Sam (D)	7th District
Goss, Porter (R)	13th District
Grant, Bill (D)	2nd District
Hutto, Earl (D)	1st District
Ireland, Andy (D)	10th District
James, Craig T (R)	4th District
Johnston, Harry (D)	14th District
Lehman, William (D)	17th District
Lewis, Tom (R)	12th District
McCollum, Bill (R)	5th District
Nelson, Bill (D)	11th District
Pepper, Claude (D)	18th District
Shaw, E Clay, Jr. (R)	15th District
Smith, Larry (D)	16th District
Stearns, Cliff (R)	6th District
Young, C. W. (R)	8th District

39

GEORGIA

Nunn, Sam (D)	Term - 1991
Fowler, Wyche Jr (D)	Term - 1993
Barnard, Doug, Jr. (D)	10th District
Darden, George (D)	7th District
Gingrich, Newt (R)	6th District
Hatcher, Charles (D)	2nd District
Jenkins, Ed (D)	9th District
Jones, Ben (D)	4th District
Lewis, John (D)	5th District
Ray, Richard (D)	3rd District
Rowland, J Roy (D)	8th District
Thomas, Lindsay (D)	1st District

HAWAII

Inouye, Daniel K. (D)	Term - 1993
Matsunaga, Spark (D)	Term - 1995
Akaka, Daniel K. (D)	2nd District
Saiki, Patricia (R)	1st District

IDAHO

McClure, James (R)	Term - 1991
Symms, Steven D. (R)	Term - 1993
Craig, Larry E (R)	1st District
Stallings, Rich (D)	2nd District

ILLINOIS

Dixon, Alan J. (D)	Term - 1993
Simon, Paul (D)	Term - 1991
Annunzio, Frank (D)	11th District
Bruce, Terry (D)	19th District
Collins, Cardiss (D)	7th District
Costello, Jerry (D)	21st District
Crane, Philip M. (R)	12th District
Durbin, Richard J (D)	20th District
Evans, Lane (D)	17th District
Fawell, Harris W. (R)	13th District
Hastert, Dennis (R)	14th District
Hayes, Charles A (D)	1st District
Hyde, Henry J. (R)	6th District
Lipinski, William (D)	5th District
Madigan, Edward R. (R)	15th District
Martin, Lynn (R)	16th District
Michel, Robert H. (R)	18th District
Porter, John (R)	10th District
Poshard, Glenn (D)	22nd District
Rostenkowski, Dan (D)	8th District
Russo, Martin (D)	3rd District
Sangmeister, George (D)	4th District
Savage, Gus (D)	2nd District
Yates, Sidney R. (D)	9th District

INDIANA

Coats, Dan (R)	Term - 1993
Lugar, Richard G. (R)	Term - 1995
Burton, Dan (R)	6th District
Coats, Dan (R)	4th District
Hamilton, Lee H. (D)	9th District
Hiler, John (R)	3rd District
Jacobs, Andrew, Jr. (D)	10th District
Jontz, James (D)	5th District
McCloskey, Frank (D)	8th District
Myers, John T. (R)	7th District
Sharp, Philip R. (D)	2nd District
Visclosky, Peter (D)	1st District

IOWA

Grassley, Charles E. (R)	Term - 1993
Harkin, Tom (D)	Term - 1991
Grandy, Fred (R)	6th District
Leach, James A.S. (R)	1st District
Lightfoot, J R (R)	5th District
Nagle, David (D)	3rd District
Smith, Neal (D)	4th District
Tauke, Thomas (R)	2nd District

KANSAS

Dole, Robert (R)	Term - 1993
Kassebaum, Nancy (R)	Term - 1991
Glickman, Dan (D)	4th District
Meyers , Jan (R)	3rd District
Roberts, Pat (R)	1st District
Slattery, Jim (D)	2nd District
Whittaker, Robert (R)	5th District

KENTUCKY

Ford, Wendell, H. (D)	Term - 1993
McConnell, A. M. (R)	Term - 1991
Bunning, Jim (R)	4th District
Hopkins, Larry (R)	6th District
Hubbard, Carroll, Jr. (D)	1st District
Mazzoli, Romano L. (D)	3rd District
Natcher, William H. (D)	2nd District
Perkins, Carl D. (D)	7th District
Rogers, Harold (R)	5th District

LOUISIANA

Johnston, J. Bennett (D)	Term - 1991
Breaux, John B. (D)	Term 1993
Boggs, Lindy Hill (D)	2nd District
Baker, Richard (R)	6th District
Hayes, James (D)	7th District
Holloway, Clyde C (R)	8th District

Huckaby, Jerry (D)	5th District
Livingston, Bob (R)	1st District
McCrery, Jim (R)	4th District
Tauzin, Billy (D)	3rd District

MAINE
Cohen, William S. (R)	Term - 1991
Mitchell, George (D)	Term - 1995
Brennan, Joseph (D)	1st District
Snowe, Olympia (R)	2nd District

MARYLAND
Sarbanes, Paul S. (D)	Term - 1995
Mikulski, Barbara (D)	Term - 1993
Bentley, H. Delich (R)	2nd District
Byron, Beverly B. (D)	6th District
Cardin, Benjamin (D)	3rd District
Dyson, Royden (D)	1st District
Hoyer, Stenyh (D)	5th District
McMillen, Tom (D)	4th District
Mfume, Kweisi (D)	7th District
Morella, Constance (R)	8th District

MASSACHUSETTS
Kennedy, Edw M. (D)	Term - 1993
Kerry, John (D)	Term - 1991
Atkins, Chester G. (D)	5th District
Conte, Silvio O. (R)	1st District
Donnelly, Brian (D)	11th District
Early, Joseph (D)	3rd District
Frank, Barney (D)	4th District
Kennedy, Joseph (D)	8th District
Markey, Edward J. (D)	7th District
Mavroules, Nicholas (D)	6th District
Moakley, Joe (D)	9th District
Neal, Richard E (D)	2nd District
Studds, Gerry E. (D)	10th District

MICHIGAN
Levin, Carl M. (D)	Term - 1991
Riegle, Donald W. (D)	Term - 1995
Bonior, David E. (D)	12th District
Broomfield, Wm S (R)	18th District
Carr, Bob (D)	6th District
Conyers, John Jr. (D)	1st District
Crockett, George (D)	13th District
Davis, Robert (R)	11th District
Dingell, John D. (D)	16th District
Ford, William D. (D)	15th District
Henry, Paul B. (R)	5th District

Hertel, Dennis (D)	14th District
Jagt Vander, Guy (R)	9th District
Kildee, Dale E. (D)	7th District
Levin, Sander (D)	17th District
Pursell, Carl D (R)	2nd District
Schuette, Bill (R)	10th District
Traxler, Bob (D)	8th District
Upton, Fred (R)	4th District
Wolpe, Howard (D)	3rd District

MINNESOTA
Boschwitz, Rudy (R)	Term - 1995
Durenberger, Dave (R)	Term - 1993
Frenzel, Bill (R)	3rd District
Oberstar, James L (D)	8th District
Penny, Timothy J (D)	1st District
Sabo, Martin (D)	5th District
Sikorski, Gerry (D)	6th District
Stangeland, Arlen (R)	7th District
Vento, Bruce F. (D)	4th District
Weber, Vin (R)	2nd District

MISSISSIPPI
Cochran, Thad (R)	Term - 1993
Lott, Trent (R)	Term - 1995
Espy, Michael (D)	2nd District
Montgomery, G.V. (D)	3rd District
Parker, Mike (D)	4th District
Smith, Larkin I (R)	5th District
Whitten, Jamie L. (D)	1st District

MISSOURI
Danforth, John C. (R)	Term - 1995
Bond, Christopher (R)	Term - 1993
Buechner, Jack (R)	2nd District
Clay, William (Bill) (D)	1st District
Coleman, Thomas (R)	6th District
Emerson, Bill (R)	8th District
Gephardt, Richard (D)	3rd District
Hancock, Melton D (R)	7th District
Skelton, Ike (D)	4th District
Volkmer, Harold L. (D)	9th District
Wheat, Alan (D)	5th District

MONTANA
Baucus, Max (D)	Term - 1991
Burns, Conrad (R)	Term - 1995
Marlenee, Ron (R)	2nd District
Williams, Pat (D)	1st District

NEBRASKA
Exon, James J. (D) — Term - 1991
Kerrey, Bob (D) — Term - 1995
Bereuter, Douglas (R) — 1st District
Hoagland, Peter (D) — 2nd District
Smith, Virginia (R) — 3rd District

NEVADA
Bryan, Richard (D) — Term - 1995
Reid, Harry (D) — Term - 1993
Bilbray, James (D) — 1st District
Vucanovich, Barbara (R) — 2nd District

NEW HAMPSHIRE
Humphrey, Gordon (R) — Term - 1995
Rudman, Warren (R) — Term - 1993
Douglas, Chuck (R) — 2nd District
Smith, Robert C. (R) — 1st District

NEW JERSEY
Bradley, Bill (D) — Term - 1991
Lautenberg, Frank (D) — Term - 1995
Courter, Jim (R) — 12th District
Dwyer, Bernard (D) — 6th District
Florio, James J. (D) — 1st District
Gallo, Dean A. (R) — 11th District
Guarini, Frank J. (D) — 14th District
Hughes, William J. (D) — 2nd District
Pallone, Frank (D) — 3rd District
Payne, Donald (D) — 10th District
Rinaldo, Matthew J. (R) — 7th District
Roe, Robert A. (D) — 8th District
Roukema, Marge (R) — 5th District
Saxton, James H. (R) — 13th District
Smith, Christopher (R) — 4th District
Torricelli, Robert (D) — 9th District

NEW MEXICO
Bingaman, Jeff (D) — Term - 1995
Domenici, Pete V. (R) — Term - 1993
Richardson, Bill (D) — 3rd District
Schiff, Steven (R) — 1st District
Skeen, Joseph R. (R) — 2nd District

NEW YORK
Moynihan, Daniel P (D) — Term - 1995
D'Amato, Alfonse M (R) — Term - 1993
Ackerman, Gary (D) — 7th District
Boehlert, Sherwood (R) — 25th District
Downey, Thomas J. (D) — 2nd District
Engel, Eliot (D) — 19th District
Fish, Hamilton, Jr. (R) — 21st District

NEW YORK Continued
Flake, Floyd (D) — 6th District
Garcia, Robert (D) — 18th District
Gilman, Benjamin (R) — 22nd District
Green, S. Wm. (R) — 15th District
Hochbrueckner G. (D) — 1st District
Horton, Frank (R) — 29th District
Houghton, Amory (R) — 34th District
La Falce, John J. (D) — 32nd District
Lent, Norman F. (R) — 4th District
Lowey, Nita (D) — 20th District
Manton, Thomas J (D) — 9th District
Martin, David (R) — 26th District
McGrath, R. J (R) — 5th District
McHugh, Matthew (D) — 28th District
McNulty, Michael (D) — 23rd District
Molinari, Guy (R) — 14th District
Mrazek, Robert J (D) — 3rd District
Nowak, Henry J. (D) — 33rd District
Owens, Major R (D) — 12th District
Paxon, Bill (R) — 31st District
Rangel, Charles B. (D) — 16th District
Scheuer, James H. (D) — 8th District
Schumer, Charles (D) — 10th District
Slaughter, Louise (D) — 30th District
Solarz, Stephen J. (D) — 13th District
Solomon, Gerald (R) — 24th District
Towns, Edolphus (D) — 11th District
Walsh, James (R) — 27th District
Weiss, Theodore S. (D) — 17th District

NORTH CAROLINA
Helms, Jesse A. (R) — Term - 1991
Sanford, Terry (D) — Term - 1993
Ballenger, Cass (R) — 10th District
Coble, Howard (R) — 6th District
Clark, Jaime (D) — 11th District
Hefner, W.G. (Bill) (D) — 8th District
Jones, Walter B. (D) — 1st District
Lancaster, Martin (D) — 3rd District
McMillan, Alex (R) — 9th District
Neal, Stephen L. (D) — 5th District
Price, David (D) — 4th District
Rose, Charles III (D) — 7th District
Valentine, I. Tim (D) — 2nd District

NORTH DAKOTA
Burdick, Quentin N (D) — Term - 1995
Conrad, Kent (D) — Term - 1993
Dorgan, Byron (D) — At Large

OHIO

Glenn, John (D)	Term - 1993
Metzenbaum, H. (D)	Term - 1995
Applegate, Douglas (D)	18th District
De Wine, Michael (R)	7th District
Eckart, Dennis (D)	11th District
Feighan, Edward F (D)	19th District
Gillmor, Paul E (R)	5th District
Gradison, Willis, Jr. (R)	2nd District
Hall, Tony P. (D)	3rd District
Kaptur, Marcy (D)	9th District
Kasich, John R (R)	12th District
Luken, Thomas A (D)	1st District
Lukens, Donald E (R)	8th District
McEwen, Bob (R)	6th District
Miller, Clarence E. (R)	10th District
Oakar, Mary Rose (D)	20th District
Oxley, Michael G (R)	4th District
Pease, Donald J. (D)	13th District
Regula, Ralph S. (R)	16th District
Sawyer, Thomas (D)	14th District
Stokes, Louis (D)	21st District
Traficant, J. A., Jr. (R)	17th District
Wylie, Chalmers P. (R)	15th District

OKLAHOMA

Boren, David (D)	Term - 1991
Nickles, Don (R)	Term - 1993
Edwards, Mickey (R)	5th District
English, Glenn (D)	6th District
Inhofe, James (R)	1st District
McCurdy, David (D)	4th District
Synar, Mike (D)	2nd District
Watkins, Wes (D)	3rd District

OREGON

Hatfield, Mark O. (R)	Term - 1991
Packwood, Bob (R)	Term - 1993
AuCoin, Les (D)	1st District
DeFazio, Peter (D)	4th District
Smith, Denny (R)	5th District
Smith, Robert (R)	2nd District
Wyden, Ron (D)	3rd District

PENNSYLVANIA

Heinz, H. John III (R)	Term - 1995
Specter, Arlen (R)	Term - 1993
Borski, Robert A. (D)	3rd District
Clinger, William, Jr. (R)	23rd District
Coughlin, Lawrence (R)	13th District

PENNSYLVANIA Continued

Coyne, William (D)	14th District
Fogiletta, Thomas (D)	1st District
Gaydos, Joseph M. (D)	20th District
Gekas, George W. (R)	17th District
Goodling, William F (R)	19th District
Gray, William H. III (D)	2nd District
Kanjorski, Paul E (D)	11th District
Kolter, Joseph P. (D)	4th District
Kosmayer, Peter H (D)	8th District
McDade, Joseph M (R)	10th District
Murphy, Austin J. (D)	22nd District
Murtha, John P. (D)	12th District
Ridge, Thomas J. (R)	21st District
Ritter, Donald (R)	15th District
Schulze, Richard T. (R)	5th District
Shuster, Bud (R)	9th District
Walgren, Doug (D)	18th District
Walker, Robert S. (R)	16th District
Weldon, Curt (R)	7th District
Yatron, Gus (D)	6th District

RHODE ISLAND

Chafee, John H. (R)	Term - 1995
Pell, Claiborne, (D)	Term - 1991
Machtley, Ronald (R)	1st District
Schneider, C. (R)	2nd District

SOUTH CAROLINA

Hollings, Ernest F. (D)	Term - 1993
Thurmond, Strom (R)	Term - 1991
Derrick, Butler (D)	3rd District
Patterson, Elizabeth (D)	4th District
Ravenel, Arthur (R)	1st District
Spence, Floyd (R)	2nd District
Spratt, John (D)	5th District
Tallon, Robin (D)	6th District

SOUTH DAKOTA

Pressler, Larry (R)	Term 1991
Daschle, Thomas (D)	Term 1993
Johnson, Timothy (D)	At Large

TENNESSEE

Gore, Albert, Jr. (D)	Term - 1991
Sasser, James R. (D)	Term - 1995
Clement, Bob (D)	5th District
Cooper, James (D)	4th District
Duncan, John Jr (R)	2nd District
Ford, Harold E. (D)	9th District
Gordon, Bart (D)	6th District

TENNESSEE Continued

Lloyd, Marilyn (D)	3rd District
Quillen, James H. (R)	1st District
Sundquist, Don (R)	7th District
Tanner, John (D)	8th District

TEXAS

Bentsen, Lloyd (D)	Term - 1995
Gramm, Phil (R)	Term - 1991
Andrews, Mike (D)	25th District
Archer, Bill (R)	7th District
Armey, Richard (R)	26th District
Bartlett, Steve (R)	3rd District
Barton, Joe (R)	6th District
Brooks, Jack (D)	9th District
Bryant, John (D)	5th District
Bustamente, A. G. (D)	23rd District
Chapman, Jim (D)	1st District
Coleman, Ronald (D)	16th District
Combest, Larry (R)	19th District
de la Garza, E. (D)	15th District
DeLay, Tom (R)	22nd District
Fields, Jack (R)	8th District
Frost, Martin (D)	24th District
Gonzalez, Henry B (D)	20th District
Hall, Ralph (D)	4th District
Laughlin, Greg (D)	14th District
Leath, Marvin (D)	11th District
Leland, Mickey (D)	18th District
Ortiz, Solomon P (D)	27th District
Pickle, J. J. (D)	10th District
Sarpalius, Bill (D)	13th District
Smith Lamar (R)	21st District
Stenholm, Charles (D)	17th District
Wilson, Charles (D)	2nd District
Wright, Jim (D)	12th District

UTAH

Garn, Jake (R)	Term - 1993
Hatch, Orrin G. (R)	Term - 1995
Hansen, James (R)	1st District
Neilson, Howard C (R)	3rd District
Owens, Wayne (D)	2nd District

VERMONT

Leahy, Patrick J. (D)	Term - 1993
Jeffords, James M. (R)	Term - 1995
Smith Peter (R)	At-Large

VIRGINIA

Robb, Charles (D)	Term - 1995
Warner, John W. (R)	Term - 1991
Bateman, Herbert H. (R)	1st District
Bliley, Thomas (R)	3rd District
Boucher, Frederick C (D)	9th District
Olin, James R (D)	6th District
Parris, Stanford (R)	8th District
Payne, Lewis F (D)	5th District
Pickett, Owen (D)	2nd District
Sisisky, Norman (D)	4th District
Slaughter, D French (R)	7th District
Wolf, Frank (R)	10th District

WASHINGTON

Gorton, Slade (R)	Term - 1995
Adams, Brock (D)	Term - 1993
Chandler, Rod (R)	8th District
Dicks, Norman D. (D)	6th District
Foley, Thomas S. (D)	5th District
McDermott, James (D)	7th District
Miller, John (R)	1st District
Morrison, Sid (R)	4th District
Swift, Al (D)	2nd District
Unsoeld, Jolene (D)	3rd District

WEST VIRGINIA

Byrd, Robert C. (D)	Term - 1995
Rockefeller, J D IV (D)	Term - 1991
Mollohan, Alan B (D)	1st District
Rahall, Nick Joe II (D)	4th District
Staggers, Harley O (D)	2nd District
Wise Jr, Robert (D)	3rd District

WISCONSIN

Kasten, Robert W. Jr. (R)	Term - 1993
Kohl, Herbert H (D)	Term - 1995
Aspin, Les (D)	1st District
Gunderson, S. (R)	3rd District
Kastenmeier, Robert (D)	2nd District
Kleczka, Gerald D. (D)	4th District
Moody, James (D)	5th District
Obey, David R (D)	7th District
Petri, Thomas (R)	6th District
Roth, Tobias (R)	8th District
Sensenbrenner, Jas (R)	9th District

WYOMING

Simpson, Alan K. (R)	Term - 1991
Wallop, Malcolm (R)	Term - 1995
Cheney, Richard (R)	At Large

THE CAPITOL
Second Floor Plan

The Senate

1 Official Reporters of Debates
2 President's Room
3 The Marble Room
4 Formal Office of the Vice President
5 Reception Room
6 Office of the Vice President
7 Bill Clerk and Journal Clerk
8 Senators' Private Lobby
9 Chief Clerk
10 Secretary
11 Cloakrooms
12 Grand Staircase
13 Senate Majority Leader's Office
14 Senate Conference Room
15 Senate Minority Leader's Office
16 Executive Clerk
17-22 Senators' Private Offices
23 Senate Disbursing Office
24 Small Senate Rotunda
25 Senate Minority Whip
26-31 Senators' Private Offices

EAST FRONT

© FLASHMAPS PUBLICATIONS Inc.

The House

32 House Minority Leader's Office
33 Prayer Room
34 Representative's Private Office
35 House Majority Conference Room
36 House Minority Conference Room
37 House Subcommittee on Foreign Affairs
38 Congressional Ladies Reading Room
39 House Document Room
40 Office of the Speaker
41 House Reception Room
42 House Minority Whip
43 Committee on Ways and Means
44 Grand Staircase
45 Cloakrooms
46 Committee on Appropriations
47 Library
48 Members' Reading Rooms
49 Parliamentarian
50 Formal Office of the Speaker

Open to the Public

Two flags fly 24 hours a day over East and West Front (central part)

Tholus (top of dome) has lights that indicate if either house is sitting.

Flags that indicate which house is in session fly over wing of house in session.

The Supreme Court Justices: William H. Rhenquist, Chief Justice

William J. Brennan, Jr.	Harry A. Blackmun	Sandra Day O'Connor
Byron R. White	Lewis F. Powell, Jr	Antonin Scalia
Thurgood Marshall	John P. Stevens	

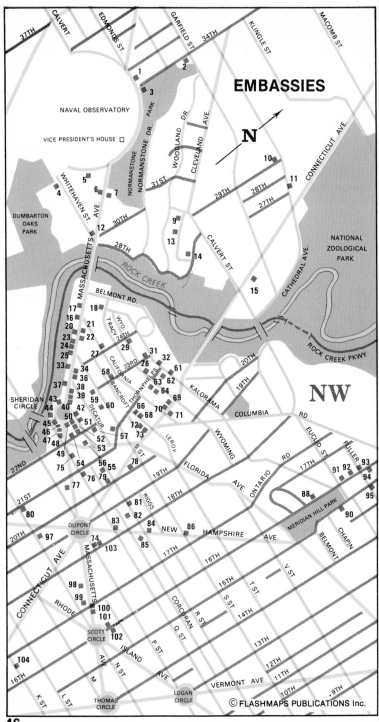

EMBASSIES

N

NW

© FLASHMAPS PUBLICATIONS Inc.

46

EMBASSIES— BY MAP NUMBER

1	Cape Verde	24	Paraguay	51	Guatemala	79	Costa Rica
1	Norway	25	Madagascar	52	Tanzania	80	Nigeria
2	Belgium	26	Algeria	53	Niger	80	St. Lucia
3	Vatican	26	Syria	54	Bulgaria	81	Sierra Leone
4	Denmark	27	Yugoslavia	54	Central Africa	82	Singapore
5	New Zealand	29	Afghanistan	55	Chad	83	Argentina
6	Great Britain	31	Thailand	56	Mali	84	Grenada
7	South Africa	32	USSR	57	Dominican Rep	84	Rwanda
9	Panama	33	Malaysia	58	El Salvador	85	Nicaragua
10	Switzerland	34	Cameroon	59	Burma	86	Zaire
11	Benin	36	Austria	60	Laos	88	Ghana
12	Bolivia	37	Oman	62	Ethiopia	90	Ecuador
12	Brazil	37	Upper Volta	63	Sri Lanka	91	Lithuania
13	Zimbabwe	38	Pakistan	64	Barbados	92	Poland
14	Lebanon	39	Haiti	66	Nepal	93	Italy
15	China	40	Egypt	68	Mauritania	94	Mexico
16	Canada	42	Kenya	69	Senegal	95	Spain
17	Japan	43	Korea	70	Iceland	97	Mozambique
17	Lesotho	44	Turkey	71	Malta	98	Chile
18	Guyana	45	Romania	72	Colombia	98	Germany (East)
18	Portugal	46	Ireland	73	Guinea	99	Trinidad
20	Ivory Coast	47	Luxembourg	74	Iraq	99	Tobago
21	Venezuela	48	Sudan	75	India	100	Peru
22	Zambia	48	Togo	76	Morocco	101	Philippines
23	Tunisia	49	Greece	77	Indonesia	102	Australia
24	Malawi	50	Cyprus	78	Gabon	104	Jamaica

EMBASSIES

Embassy	Address	Map No	Telephone
Afghanistan	2341 Wyoming Avenue NW	29	234-3770
Algeria	2137 Wyoming Avenue NW	26	328-5300
Argentina	1600 New Hampshire NW	83	939-6400
Australia	1601 Massachusetts NW	102	797-3000
Austria	2343 Massachusetts NW	36	483-4474
Bahamas	600 New Hampshire NW	★	944-3390
Bahrain	3502 International Drive NW	★	342-0741
Bangladesh	2201 Wisconsin Ave NW	★	342-8372
Barbados	2144 Wyoming Ave NW	64	939-9200
Belgium	3330 Garfield Street NW	2	333-6900
Benin	2737 Cathedral Ave	11	232-6656
Bolivia	3014 Massachusetts NW	12	483-4410
Botswana	4301 Connecticut Ave NW	★	244-4990
Brazil	3006 Massachusetts NW	12	745-2700
Bulgaria	1621 22nd Street NW	54	387-7969
Burma	2300 S Street NW	59	332-9044
Burundi	2233 Wisconsin Ave NW	★	342-2574
Cameroon	2349 Massachusetts NW	34	265-8790
Canada	2450 Massachusetts NW	16	483-5505
Cape Verde	3415 Massachusetts NW	1	965-6820
Central Africa Republic	1618 22nd Street NW	54	483-7800
Chad	2002 R Street NW	55	462-4009
Chile	1736 Massachusetts NW	98	785-1746
China, People's Rep	2300 Connecticut Ave NW	15	328-2500
Colombia	2118 Leroy Place NW	72	387-8338
Congo	4891 Colorado Ave NW	★	726-5500

★ off map

Embassy	Address	Map No	Telephone
Costa Rica	1825 Conn Ave NW	79	234-2945
Cyprus	2211 R Street NW	50	462-5772
Czechoslovakia	3900 Linnean Ave NW	*	363-6315
Denmark	3200 Whitehaven Street NW	4	234-4300
Dominican Republic	1715 22nd Street NW	57	332-6280
Ecuador	2535 15th Street NW	90	234-7200
Egypt	2310 Decatur Place NW	40	232-5400
El Salvador	2308 California StreetNW	58	265-3480
Ethiopia	2134 Kalorama Road NW	62	234-2281
Fiji	2233 Wisconsin Ave NW	*	337-8320
Finland	3216 New Mexico Ave NW	*	363-2430
France	4101 Reservoir Road NW	*	944-6000
Gabon	2034 20th Street NW	78	797-1000
German Dem Rep (East)	1717 Massachusetts Ave NW	98	232-3134
German Fed Rep (West)	4645 Reservoir Road NW	*	298-4000
Ghana	2460 16th Street NW	88	462-0761
Great Britain	3100 Massachusetts NW	6	462-1340
Greece	2221 Massachusetts NW	49	667-3168
Grenada	1701 New Hampshire NW	84	265-2561
Guatemala	2220 R Street NW	51	745-4952
Guinea	2112 Leroy Place NW	73	483-9420
Guyana	2490 Tracy Place NW	18	265-6900
Haiti	2311 Massachusetts NW	39	332-4090
Honduras	4301 Connecticut NW	*	966-7700
Hungary	3910 Shoemaker St NW	*	362-6730
Iceland	2022 Connecticut NW	70	265-6653
India	2107 Massachusetts NW	75	939-7000
Indonesia	2020 Massachusetts NW	77	775-5200
Iraq	1801 P Street NW	74	483-7500
Ireland	2234 Massachusetts NW	46	462-3939
Israel	3514 International Dr NW	*	364-5500
Italy	1601 Fuller Street NW	93	328-5500
Ivory Coast	2424 Massachusetts NW	20	483-2400
Jamaica	1850 K Street NW	104	452-0660
Japan	2520 Massachusetts NW	17	234-2266
Jordan	3504 International Dr NW	*	966-2664
Kenya	2249 R Street NW	42	387-6101
Korea	2320 Massachusetts NW	43	939-5600
Kuwait	2940 Tilden Street NW	*	966-0702
Laos	2222 S Street NW	60	332-6416
Latvia	4325 17th Street NW	*	726-8213
Lebanon	2560 28th Street NW	14	939-6300
Lesotho	2511 Massachusetts NW	17	797-5533
Liberia	5201 16th Street NW	*	723-0437
Lithuania	2622 16th Street NW	91	234-5860
Luxembourg	2200 Massachusetts NW	47	265-4171
Madagascar	2374 Massachusetts NW	25	265-5525
Malawi	2408 Massachusetts NW	24	797-1007
Malaysia	2401 Massachusetts NW	33	328-2700
Mali	2130 R Street NW	56	332-2249
Malta	2017 Connecticut NW	71	462-3611
Mauritania	2129 Leroy Place NW	68	232-5700
Mauritius	4301 Connecticut NW	*	244-1491
Mexico	2829 16th Street NW	94	234-6000

　　　　　　　　　　　　　　　　　　　　　* off map

EMBASSIES (Continued)

Embassy	Address	Map No	Telephone
Morocco	1601 21st Street NW	76	462-7979
Mozambique	1990 M Street NW	97	293-7146
Nepal	2131 Leroy Place NW	66	667-4550
Netherlands	4200 Linnean Ave NW	*	244-5300
New Zealand	37 Observatory Circle NW	5	328-4800
Nicaragua	1627 New Hampshire NW	85	387-4371
Niger	2204 R Street NW	53	483-4224
Nigeria	2201 M Street NW	80	822-1500
Norway	2720 34th Street NW	1	333-6000
Oman	2342 Massachusetts NW	37	387-1980
Pakistan	2315 Massachusetts NW	38	939-6200
Panama	2862 McGill Terrace NW	9	483-1407
Paraguay	2400 Massachusetts NW	24	483-6960
Peru	1700 Massachusetts NW	100	833-9860
Philippines	1617 Massachusetts NW	101	483-1414
Poland	2640 16th Street NW	92	234-3800
Portugal	2310 Tracy Pl NW	18	332-3007
Qatar	600 New Hampshire NW	*	338-0111
Romania	1607 23rd Street NW	45	232-4747
Rwanda	1714 New Hampshire NW	84	232-2882
San Marino	1155 21st Street NW	*	223-3517
Saudi Arabia	601 New Hampshire NW	*	342-3800
Senegal	2112 Wyoming Ave NW	69	234-0540
Sierra Leone	1701 19th Street NW	81	939-9261
Singapore	1824 R Street NW	82	667-7555
Somalia	600 New Hampshire NW	*	342-1575
South Africa	3051 Massachusetts NW	7	232-4400
Spain	2700 15th Street NW	95	265-0190
Sri Lanka	2148 Wyoming Ave NW	63	483-4025
St. Lucia	2100 M Street NW	80	463-7378
Sudan	2210 Massachusetts NW	48	466-6280
Surinam	4301 Connecticut NW	*	244-7488
Swaziland	4301 Connecticut NW	*	362-6683
Sweden	600 New Hampshire NW	*	944-5600
Switzerland	2900 Cathedral Ave NW	10	745-7900
Syria	2215 Wyoming NW	26	232-6313
Tanzania	2139 R Street NW	52	939-6125
Thailand	2300 Kalorama Road NW	31	483-7200
Togo	2208 Massachusetts NW	48	234-4212
Trinidad/Tobago	1708 Massachusetts NW	99	467-6490
Tunisia	1515 Massachusetts NW	23	862-1850
Turkey	1606 23rd Street NW	44	387-3200
Uganda	5909 16th Street NW	*	726-7100
United Arab Emirates	600 New Hampshire NW	*	338-6500
Upper Volta	2340 Massachusetts NW	37	332-5577
Uruguay	1918 F Street NW	*	331-1313
U. S. S. R.	1825 Phelps NW	32	628-7551
Vatican	3339 Massachusetts NW	3	333-7121
Venezuela	2445 Massachusetts NW	21	797-3800
Yemen	600 New Hampshire NW	*	965-4760
Yugoslavia	2410 California Street NW	27	462-6566
Zaire	1800 New Hampshire NW	86	234-7690
Zambia	2419 Massachusetts NW	22	265-9717
Zimbabwe	2852 McGill Terrace NW	13	332-7100

* off map

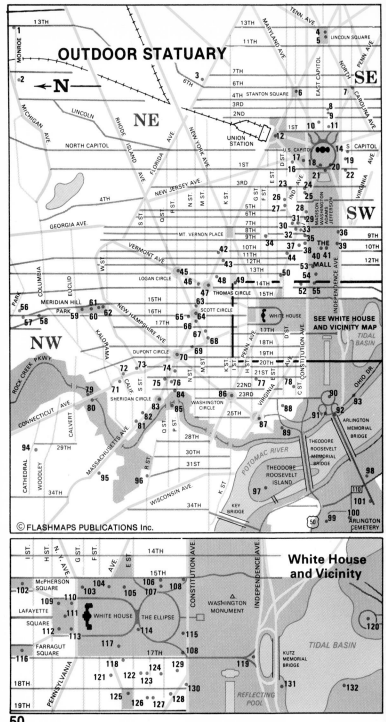

OUTDOOR STATUARY

← N →

NE

SE

SW

NW

White House and Vicinity

© FLASHMAPS PUBLICATIONS Inc.

50

OUTDOOR STATUARY — BY MAP NUMBERS

1 St. Jerome, the Priest	48 Christ, Light of World	94 Eurythmy
2 St. Dominic	49 Commodore J. Barry	94 Orbit
3 Thomas Gaullaudet	50 Gen. Count Pulaski	95 Winston Churchill
3 Edward Gaullaudet	52 Strauss Fountain	96 Pebble Garden
4 Mary McLeod Bethune	53 Three Red Lines	97 Theodore Roosevelt
5 Emancipation Monument	54 Infinity	98 The Hiker
6 Gen. Nathanael Greene	55 The Gwenfritz	99 Marine Corps Mem
7 Olive Risley Seward	56 Cardinal Gibbons	100 Netherlands Carillon
8 Shakespeare Scenes	57 Marconi Memorial	101 Rear Adm. Richrd Byrd
9 Puck Fountain	58 Francis Asbury	102 Gen. James McPherson
10 Law & Justice	59 Serenity	103 Albert Gallatin
11 The Court of Neptune	60 Dante	104 Alexander Hamilton
11 Ethnological Heads	61 Joan of Arc	105 Gen W. T. Sherman
12 Columbus Fountain	62 James Buchanan	106 Settlers of D.C.
14 Greek Vases	63 Dr. Samuel Hahnemann	107 Boys Scout Memorial
16 Acacia Griffins	64 Gen. Winfield Scott	108 Bullfinch Gatehouses
17 Taft Memorial	65 Australian Seal	109 Gen. Kosciuszko
18 Peace Monument	66 Daniel Webster	110 Gen. Lafayette
19 Law & Justice	67 Nuns of Battlefield	111 Andrew Jackson
20 Pres. James Garfield	68 H. W. Longfellow	112 Baron von Steuben
21 U.S. Grant Memorial	69 John Witherspoon	113 Comte de Rochambeau
22 Bartholdi Fountain	70 Dupont Memorial-	114 Butt-Millet Memorial
23 Gen. Albert Pike	Daniel Chester French	115 2nd Div. Memorial
24 Blackstone	71 Habitat	116 Adm David Farragut
25 Trylon of Freedom	72 Gen Geo. McClellan	117 1st Div. Memorial
26 Abraham Lincoln	73 Cubi XI	118 Canova Lions
27 Darlington Fountain	74 Balinese Demons	119 John Paul Jones
28 Mellon Fountain	75 Braque Bird	120 Jefferson Memorial
29 Man Controlling Trade	76 Hercules/Buddha/Sphinx	121 Architects Memorial
30 Temperance Fountain	77 Ascension	122 Red Cross Memorial
31 G.A.R. Memorial	78 Expanding Universe	123 Jane A Delano
32 Gen. W. S. Hancock	79 Bairstow Lampposts	124 D.A.R. Founders
33 Past & Future	80 Perry Lions	125 Gen. John Rawlins
34 Pegasus & Bellerophon	81 The Prophet	126 Negro Mother & Child
35 Acroterion Eagles	82 Robert Emmet	127 Lincoln, Rail Joiner
36 Burghers of Calais	83 Gen. Philip Sheridan	128 Gen. Simon Bolivar
37 Robert F. Kennedy	84 Taras Shevchenko	129 Queen Isabella
38 Capt. Nathan Hale	85 Buffaloes	129 South America
39 A.J. Downing Urn	86 George Washington	129 North America
40 Uncle Beazley	87 Benito Juarez	129 Aztec Fountain
41 Joseph Henry	88 Dr. Benjamin Rush	129 The Prophet Daniel
42 Sam Gompers Memorial	89 America-War & Peace	129 Jose Cecilio D'Valle
43 Edmund Burke	90 Lincoln Memorial and	129 Cordell Hull
44 Benjamin Franklin	Vietnam Veterans Mem	129 Xochipilli, Aztec God
45 Gen. John Logan	91 The Arts of Peace	130 Jose Gervasio Artigas
46 Martin Luther	92 The Arts of War	131 Japanese Lantern
47 Gen. George Thomas	93 John Ericsson	132 Japanese Pagoda

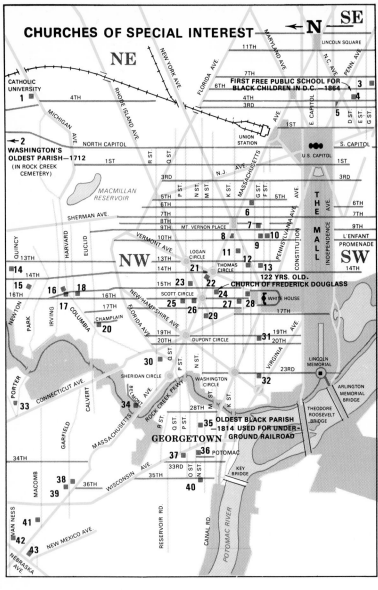

CHURCHES OF SPECIAL INTEREST

← N SE

NE

NW

SW

CATHOLIC UNIVERSITY
1

WASHINGTON'S OLDEST PARISH—1712
(IN ROCK CREEK CEMETERY)
← 2

FIRST FREE PUBLIC SCHOOL FOR BLACK CHILDREN IN D.C. — 1864
3
4
5

LINCOLN SQUARE

UNION STATION

U.S. CAPITOL

MACMILLAN RESERVOIR

THE MALL

L'ENFANT PROMENADE

LOGAN CIRCLE

THOMAS CIRCLE

122 YRS. OLD.
CHURCH OF FREDERICK DOUGLASS

SCOTT CIRCLE

WHITE HOUSE

DUPONT CIRCLE

SHERIDAN CIRCLE

WASHINGTON CIRCLE

LINCOLN MEMORIAL

ARLINGTON MEMORIAL BRIDGE

THEODORE ROOSEVELT BRIDGE

GEORGETOWN

OLDEST BLACK PARISH —1814 USED FOR UNDERGROUND RAILROAD

POTOMAC

KEY BRIDGE

POTOMAC RIVER

CHURCHES PRESIDENTS ATTENDED

3 Thomas Jefferson	28 Franklin Pierce	7 Warren Harding
28 James Madison	12 Abraham Lincoln	9 Calvin Coolidge
28 James Monroe	25 Rutherford B. Hayes	30 Herbert Hoover
28 John Quincy Adams	22 James A. Garfield	26 Harry S. Truman
28 Martin Van Buren	28 Chester A. Arthur	40 John F. Kennedy
28 Wm. Henry Harrison	23 Theodore Roosevelt	22 Lyndon Johnson
28 John Tyler	18 William H Taft	28 Gerald Ford
28 Zachary Taylor	16 Woodrow Wilson	26 Jimmy Carter

CHURCHES OF SPECIAL INTEREST—BY MAP NOS.

1	Shrine Immac	12	NY Av Presby	23	Grace Evang	34	Islamic
2	St. Paul's	13	Church Epiph	24	Metro AME	35	Mt. Zion
3	Christ Church	14	Franciscan	25	Foundry Meth	36	St. John's
4	Ebenezer	15	St. Stephen	26	First Baptist	37	G'town Luth
5	Capitol Hill	16	Central Presb	27	Third Christ	38	Cath Sophia
6	St. Mary's	17	Nat'l Baptist	28	St. John's	39	Wash Nat'l
7	Calvary Bapt	18	All Souls'	29	St. Matthew's	40	Holy Trinity
8	Mt. Vernon	19	Shiloh Baptist	30	Friends Mtg	41	Wash Hebrew
9	First Congr	20	First Christ	31	Westrn Presby	42	Nat'l Presby
10	St. Patrick's	21	Luther Mem	32	St. Mary's	43	Metro Mem
11	Asbury Meth	22	National City	33	Adas Israel		

CHURCHES OF SPECIAL INTEREST—ALPHABETICAL

Church	Address	Map No	Telephone
Adas Israel Synagogue	Conn & Porter NW	33	362-4433
All Souls Unitarian	16th & Harvard NW	18	332-5266
Asbury Methodist	11th & K St NW	11	628-0009
Calvary Baptist	8th & H St NW	7	347-8355
Capitol Hill Presbyterian	201 4th St SE	5	547-8676
Cathedral of St. Sophia	36th & Mass NW	38	333-4730
Central Presbyterian (site only)	15th & Irving NW	16	no phone
Christ Church	620 G St SE	3	547-9300
Church of the Epiphany	1317 G St NW	13	347-2635
Ebenezer United Methodist	4th & D St SE	4	544-9539
First Baptist Church	1326 16th St NW	26	387-2206
First Christ Scientist	1770 Euclid NW	20	265-1390
First Congregational	10th & G St NW	9	628-4317
Foundry Methodist	16th & Church NW	25	332-4010
Franciscan Monastery	1400 Quincy NE	14	526-6800
Friends Meeting of Washington	2111 Florida NW	30	483-3310
Georgetown Lutheran	Wisconsin & Volta Pl	37	337-9070
Grace Evangelical & Reform	15th & O St NW	23	387-3131
Holy Trinity Catholic	35th & O St NW	40	337-2840
Islamic Center Mosque	2551 Mass NW	34	332-8343
Luther Place Memorial	Thomas Circle/Vt Ave	21	667-1377
Metropolitan A.M.E.	1518 M St NW	24	331-1426
Metro Memorial Methodist	Nebraska & New Mex	43	363-4900
Mormon Temple, L.D.S.	9900 Stony Brook, Kngstn	off	*589-1435
Mt. Vernon Place Methodist	900 Mass NW	8	347-9620
Mt. Zion United Methodist	1334 29th NW	35	234-0148
National Baptist Memorial	1501 Columbia NW	17	265-1410
National City Christian	Thomas Circle/Mass Av	22	232-0323
National Presbyterian	Nebraska & Van Ness	42	537-0800
New York Ave Presbyterian	1313 New York Ave	12	393-3700
St. John's Episc-Lafayette Sq	1525 H St at 16th NW	28	347-8766
St. John's Episc-G'twn	3240 O St NW	36	338-1796
St. Mary's Catholic	727 5th NW	6	289-7770
St. Mary's Episcopal	728 23rd NW	32	333-3985
St. Matthew's Cathedral	1725 R. I. NW	29	347-3215
St. Patrick's Catholic	619 10th NW	10	347-2713
St. Paul's Rock Creek	Rock Creek Cemetery	2	726-2080
St. Stephen	16th & Newton NW	15	232-0900
Shiloh Bapist-Family Life Ctr	1510 9th St at P NW	19	232-4200
Shrine Immaculate Conception	Michigan & 4th NE	1	526-8300
Third Christ Scientist	900 16th NW	27	833-3325
Washington Cathedral	Wis & Mass NW	39	537-6200
Washington Hebrew Congreg.	Macomb & Mass NW	41	362-7100
Western Presbyterian	1906 H St NW	31	842-0068

*Area (301)

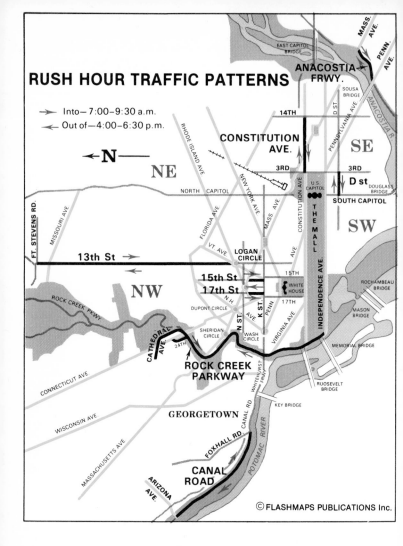

RUSH HOUR TRAFFIC PATTERNS

→ Into − 7:00−9:30 a.m.
← Out of − 4:00−6:30 p.m.

TRAFFIC INFORMATION

Parking Ticket: Fine $15.00 - $100.00
  Information for paying fine on back of ticket.
  Parking is banned during rush hours 7 to 9:30 AM and 4 to 6:30 PM
  on most downtown streets. Fine is $35.
  Cars can be towed away during these hours. Fine on the ticket
  is then doubled plus towing fee.

Tow-away fee: $25 to $35.

To retrieve car: Call Traffic Division 727-5000

Off street parking: Rates posted at every facility.
  Meter rates vary depending on location
  Minimum rates from $.25 per 1/4 hr to $1.00 per hour.

  Motor Vehicle Bureau: 727-6680 **Parking Info:** 7279208
54

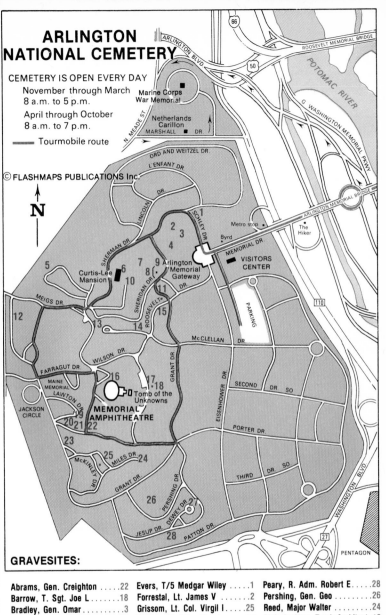

ARLINGTON NATIONAL CEMETERY

CEMETERY IS OPEN EVERY DAY

November through March
8 a.m. to 5 p.m.

April through October
8 a.m. to 7 p.m.

━━━ Tourmobile route

© FLASHMAPS PUBLICATIONS Inc.

N

Marine Corps War Memorial

Netherlands Carillon

Curtis-Lee Mansion

Arlington Memorial Gateway

VISITORS CENTER

PARKING

Tomb of the Unknowns

MEMORIAL AMPHITHEATRE

PENTAGON

POTOMAC RIVER

GRAVESITES:

55

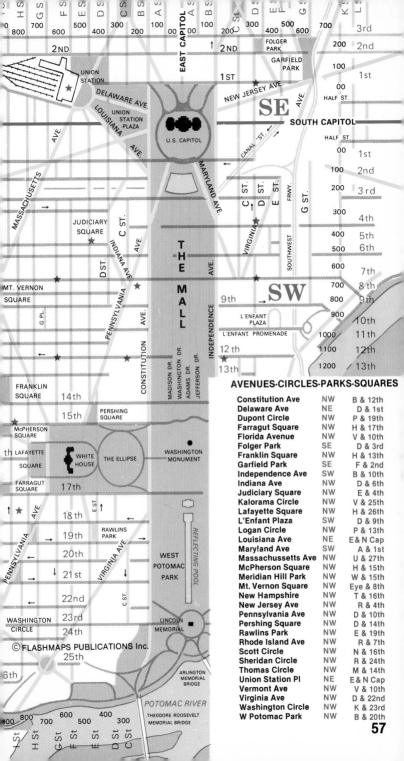

AVENUES-CIRCLES-PARKS-SQUARES

Constitution Ave	NW	B & 12th
Delaware Ave	NE	D & 1st
Dupont Circle	NW	P & 19th
Farragut Square	NW	H & 17th
Florida Avenue	NW	V & 10th
Folger Park	SE	D & 3rd
Franklin Square	NW	H & 13th
Garfield Park	SE	F & 2nd
Independence Ave	SW	B & 10th
Indiana Ave	NW	D & 6th
Judiciary Square	NW	E & 4th
Kalorama Circle	NW	V & 25th
Lafayette Square	NW	H & 26th
L'Enfant Plaza	SW	D & 9th
Logan Circle	NW	P & 13th
Louisiana Ave	NE	E & N Cap
Maryland Ave	SW	A & 1st
Massachusetts Ave	NW	U & 27th
McPherson Square	NW	H & 15th
Meridian Hill Park	NW	W & 15th
Mt. Vernon Square	NW	Eye & 8th
New Hampshire	NW	T & 16th
New Jersey Ave	NW	R & 4th
Pennsylvania Ave	NW	D & 10th
Pershing Square	NW	D & 14th
Rawlins Park	NW	E & 19th
Rhode Island Ave	NW	R & 17th
Scott Circle	NW	N & 16th
Sheridan Circle	NW	R & 24th
Thomas Circle	NW	M & 14th
Union Station Pl	NE	E & N Cap
Vermont Ave	NW	V & 10th
Virginia Ave	NW	D & 22nd
Washington Circle	NW	K & 23rd
W Potomac Park	NW	B & 20th

57

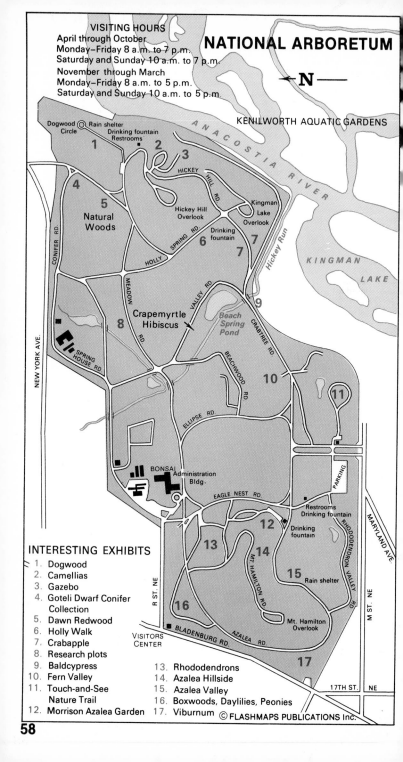

NATIONAL ARBORETUM

← **N** —

VISITING HOURS
April through October
Monday–Friday 8 a.m. to 7 p.m.
Saturday and Sunday 10 a.m. to 7 p.m.
November through March
Monday–Friday 8 a.m. to 5 p.m.
Saturday and Sunday 10 a.m. to 5 p.m.

KENILWORTH AQUATIC GARDENS

ANACOSTIA RIVER

Dogwood Circle
Rain shelter
Drinking fountain
Restrooms

1

2

3

HICKEY HILL RD.

4

5
Natural Woods

Hickey Hill Overlook

Kingman Lake Overlook

CONIFER RD.

HOLLY RD.

SPRING RD.

6

Drinking fountain

7

7

Hickey Run

KINGMAN LAKE

NEW YORK AVE.

MEADOW RD.

8

Crapemyrtle Hibiscus

VALLEY RD.

Beach Spring Pond

9

SPRING HOUSE RD.

CRABTREE RD.

BEACHWOOD RD.

10

11

ELLIPSE RD.

BONSAI
Administration Bldg.

EAGLE NEST RD.

PARKING

Restrooms
Drinking fountain

12

Drinking fountain

RHODODENDRON VALLEY

MARYLAND AVE.

INTERESTING EXHIBITS

1. Dogwood
2. Camellias
3. Gazebo
4. Goteli Dwarf Conifer Collection
5. Dawn Redwood
6. Holly Walk
7. Crabapple
8. Research plots
9. Baldcypress
10. Fern Valley
11. Touch-and-See Nature Trail
12. Morrison Azalea Garden
13. Rhododendrons
14. Azalea Hillside
15. Azalea Valley
16. Boxwoods, Daylilies, Peonies
17. Viburnum

13

14

15
Rain shelter

MT. HAMILTON RD.

16

Mt. Hamilton Overlook

R ST. NE

M ST. NE

VISITORS CENTER

BLADENBURG RD.

AZALEA RD.

17

17TH ST. NE

© FLASHMAPS PUBLICATIONS Inc.

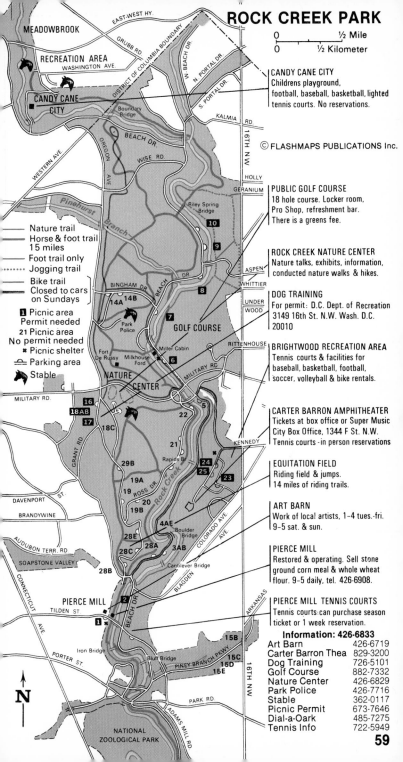

ROCK CREEK PARK

0   ½ Mile
0   ½ Kilometer

© FLASHMAPS PUBLICATIONS Inc.

CANDY CANE CITY
Childrens playground,
football, baseball, basketball, lighted
tennis courts. No reservations.

PUBLIC GOLF COURSE
18 hole course. Locker room,
Pro Shop, refreshment bar.
There is a greens fee.

ROCK CREEK NATURE CENTER
Nature talks, exhibits, information,
conducted nature walks & hikes.

DOG TRAINING
For permit: D.C. Dept. of Recreation
3149 16th St. N.W. Wash. D.C.
20010

BRIGHTWOOD RECREATION AREA
Tennis courts & facilities for
baseball, basketball, football,
soccer, volleyball & bike rentals.

CARTER BARRON AMPHITHEATER
Tickets at box office or Super Music
City Box Office, 1344 F St. N.W.
Tennis courts -in person reservations

EQUITATION FIELD
Riding field & jumps.
14 miles of riding trails.

ART BARN
Work of local artists, 1-4 tues.-fri.
9-5 sat. & sun.

PIERCE MILL
Restored & operating. Sell stone
ground corn meal & whole wheat
flour. 9-5 daily, tel. 426-6908.

PIERCE MILL TENNIS COURTS
Tennis courts can purchase season
ticket or 1 week reservation.

Information: 426-6833

Art Barn	426-6719
Carter Barron Thea	829-3200
Dog Training	726-5101
Golf Course	882-7332
Nature Center	426-6829
Park Police	426-7716
Stable	362-0117
Picnic Permit	673-7646
Dial-a-Oark	485-7275
Tennis Info	722-5949

Legend:
— Nature trail
— Horse & foot trail 15 miles
— Foot trail only
····· Jogging trail
— Bike trail Closed to cars on Sundays
1 Picnic area Permit needed
21 Picnic area No permit needed
✳ Picnic shelter
⚓ Parking area
🐎 Stable

MEADOWBROOK
RECREATION AREA
WASHINGTON AVE.
CANDY CANE CITY
EAST-WEST HY.
GRUBB RD.
DISTRICT OF COLUMBIA BOUNDARY
W. BEACH DR.
N. PORTAL DR.
S. PORTAL DR.
KALMIA RD.
16TH NW
Boundary Bridge
BEACH DR.
OREGON AVE.
WISE RD.
WESTERN AVE.
Pinehurst Branch
HOLLY
GERANIUM
ASPEN
WHITTIER
UNDER WOOD
RITTENHOUSE
Riley Spring Bridge
10
9
BINGHAM DR.
BEACH DR.
8
14A **14B**
Park Police
7
GOLF COURSE
Fort De Russy
Miller Cabin
Milkhouse Ford
6
NATURE CENTER
MILITARY RD.
MILITARY RD.
16
18AB
17
18C
5
22
KENNEDY
GRANT RD.
21
29B
Rapids Br.
24
25
23
19A
19
ROSS DR.
Rock Creek
20
19B
DAVENPORT ST.
BRANDYWINE
4AE
Boulder Bridge
COLORADO AVE.
28E
28A
3AB
28C
AUDUBON TERR. RD.
SOAPSTONE VALLEY
28B
Cantilever Bridge
BLAGDEN
CONNECTICUT AVE.
PIERCE MILL
TILDEN ST.
2
BEACH DR.
1
ARKANSAS
Iron Bridge
PORTER ST.
Bluff Bridge
PINEY BRANCH PKWY.
15B
15C
15D
15E
16TH NW
PARK RD.
ADAMS MILL RD.
NATIONAL ZOOLOGICAL PARK

N

59

NATIONAL ZOOLOGICAL PARK

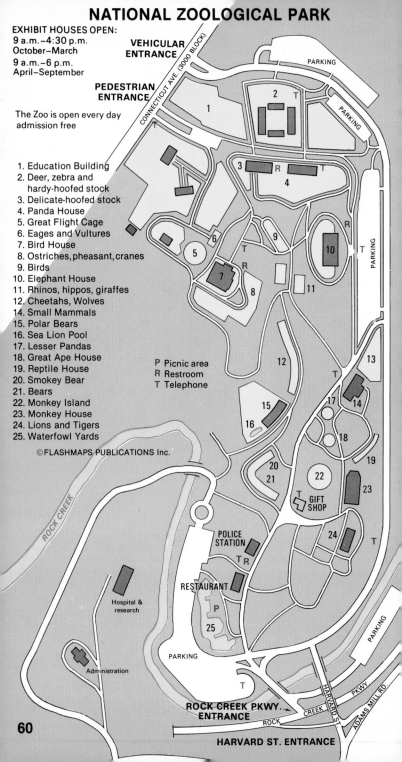

EXHIBIT HOUSES OPEN:
9 a.m.–4:30 p.m.
October–March

9 a.m.–6 p.m.
April–September

The Zoo is open every day
admission free

1. Education Building
2. Deer, zebra and
   hardy-hoofed stock
3. Delicate-hoofed stock
4. Panda House
5. Great Flight Cage
6. Eages and Vultures
7. Bird House
8. Ostriches, pheasant, cranes
9. Birds
10. Elephant House
11. Rhinos, hippos, giraffes
12. Cheetahs, Wolves
14. Small Mammals
15. Polar Bears
16. Sea Lion Pool
17. Lesser Pandas
18. Great Ape House
19. Reptile House
20. Smokey Bear
21. Bears
22. Monkey Island
23. Monkey House
24. Lions and Tigers
25. Waterfowl Yards

©FLASHMAPS PUBLICATIONS Inc.

P Picnic area
R Restroom
T Telephone

VEHICULAR ENTRANCE

PEDESTRIAN ENTRANCE

CONNECTICUT AVE. (3000 BLOCK)

PARKING

GIFT SHOP

POLICE STATION

RESTAURANT

Hospital & research

Administration

ROCK CREEK

PARKING

ROCK CREEK PKWY. ENTRANCE

HARVARD ST. ENTRANCE

HARVARD ST.

ADAMS MILL RD.

ROCK CREEK PKWY

LANDMARK DAY TRIPS
Harpers Ferry ● Mount Vernon ● Annapolis ● Wolf Trap Farm

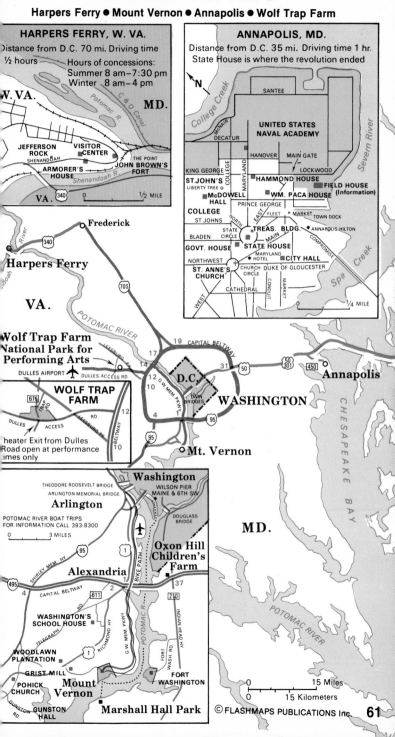

HARPERS FERRY, W. VA.
Distance from D.C. 70 mi. Driving time ½ hours
Hours of concessions:
Summer 8 am–7:30 pm
Winter 8 am–4 pm

W. VA.
MD.
C & O Canal
Potomac R.
JEFFERSON ROCK
VISITOR CENTER
SHENANDOAH
ARMORER'S HOUSE
THE POINT
JOHN BROWN'S FORT
Shenandoah R.
VA. 340
0   ½ MILE

ANNAPOLIS, MD.
Distance from D.C. 35 mi. Driving time 1 hr.
State House is where the revolution ended

N
College Creek
SANTEE
UNITED STATES NAVAL ACADEMY
MCNAIR
DECATUR
HANOVER
MAIN GATE
LOCKWOOD
Severn River
KING GEORGE
COLLEGE
MARYLAND
ST JOHN'S
HAMMOND HOUSE
LIBERTY TREE
FIELD HOUSE (Information)
McDOWELL HALL
WM. PACA HOUSE
COLLEGE
PRINCE GEORGE
ST JOHNS
FLEET
MARKET
TOWN DOCK
STATE CIRCLE
BLADEN
TREAS. BLDG.
ANNAPOLIS HILTON
MAIN
GOVT. HOUSE
STATE HOUSE
COMPROMISE
NORTHWEST
MARYLAND HOTEL
CITY HALL
ST. ANNE'S CHURCH
CHURCH CIRCLE
DUKE OF GLOUCESTER
Spa Creek
WEST
CATHEDRAL
CONDUIT
MARKET
0   ¼ MILE

Frederick
340
70S
Harpers Ferry
VA.
POTOMAC RIVER
LEESBURG PL
19 CAPITAL BELTWAY
17
14
12
10
31
50
50 301
450
Annapolis
Wolf Trap Farm National Park for Performing Arts
DULLES AIRPORT
DULLES ACCESS RD.
G W MEM PKWY
D.C.
TWIN BRIDGES
WASHINGTON
95

WOLF TRAP FARM
676
TRAP RD
DULLES ACCESS
12
BELTWAY
LEESBURG PK
RD.
10
Theater Exit from Dulles Road open at performance times only
4
95
Mt. Vernon
CHESAPEAKE BAY
MD.

Washington
THEODORE ROOSEVELT BRIDGE
ARLINGTON MEMORIAL BRIDGE
Arlington
WILSON PIER
MAINE & 6TH SW
DOUGLASS BRIDGE
POTOMAC RIVER BOAT TRIPS
FOR INFORMATION CALL 393-8300
0   3 MILES
95
1
BIKE PATH
Oxon Hill Children's Farm
Alexandria
495
CAPITAL BELTWAY
611
1
2
RICHMOND HY
G W MEM PKWY
POTOMAC R.
37
210
INDIAN HEAD HY
MD.
WASHINGTON'S SCHOOL HOUSE
TELEGRAPH RD
1
WOODLAWN PLANTATION
GRIST MILL
POHICK CHURCH
Mount Vernon
FORT WASH RD
FORT WASHINGTON
POTOMAC RIVER
GUNSTON RD
GUNSTON HALL
Marshall Hall Park
0   15 Miles
0   15 Kilometers

© FLASHMAPS PUBLICATIONS Inc.

61

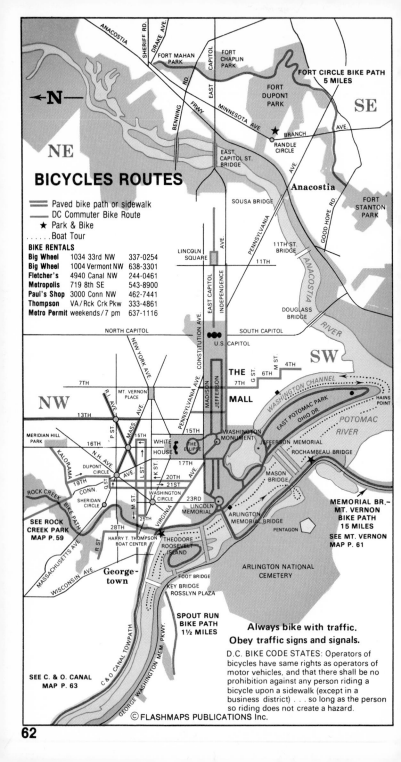

BICYCLES ROUTES

⯈N⯇

NE

SE

Paved bike path or sidewalk

DC Commuter Bike Route

★ Park & Bike

...... Boat Tour

BIKE RENTALS

Big Wheel	1034 33rd NW	337-0254
Big Wheel	1004 Vermont NW	638-3301
Fletcher's	4940 Canal NW	244-0461
Metropolis	719 8th SE	543-8900
Paul's Shop	3000 Conn NW	462-7441
Thompson	VA/Rck Crk Pkw	333-4861
Metro Permit	weekends/7 pm	637-1116

FORT CIRCLE BIKE PATH 5 MILES

MEMORIAL BR.– MT. VERNON BIKE PATH 15 MILES

SEE MT. VERNON MAP P. 61

SEE ROCK CREEK PARK MAP P. 59

SPOUT RUN BIKE PATH 1½ MILES

SEE C. & O. CANAL MAP P. 63

Always bike with traffic.
Obey traffic signs and signals.

D.C. BIKE CODE STATES: Operators of bicycles have same rights as operators of motor vehicles, and that there shall be no prohibition against any person riding a bicycle upon a sidewalk (except in a business district) ... so long as the person so riding does not create a hazard.

© FLASHMAPS PUBLICATIONS Inc.

62

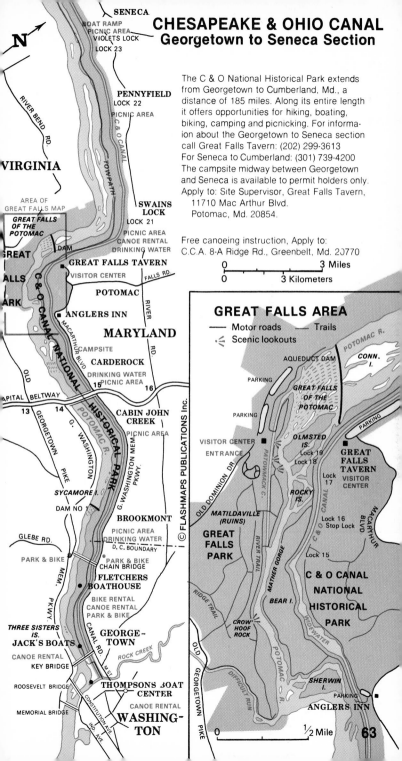

NATIONAL TREASURES—BY CATEGORY

NATIONAL TREASURES—BY CATEGORY

ART—SCULPTURE Continued

Page

French, Daniel Chester — "Lincoln"	Lincoln Memorial	18
Maillol, Aristide — "Action in Chains"	Hirshhorn Museum	18
Matisse — "Backs"	Hirshhorn Museum	18
Moore, Henry — "King and Queen"	Hirshhorn Museum	18
Moore, Henry — "Knife Edge Mirror Two Piece"	National Gallery	18
Noguchi, Isamu — "Great Rock of Inner Seeking"	National Gallery	18
Rodin — "Burghers of Calais" and "Tribute to Balzac"	Hirshhorn Mus	18
Saint-Gaudens, Augustus — "Grief"	St Paul's Church	52
Verrocchio — "Lorenzo de Medici"	National Gallery	18

ART—RARE COLLECTIONS

African Art — Sculpture and textiles	African Art Museum	76
American Antiques (Diplomatic reception rooms)	State Department	16
Byzantine and Early Christian Art	Dumbarton Oaks	76
Egyptian Gold Work	Freer Gallery	18
Japanese Screens — 17th Century	Freer Gallery	18
Judaic ceremonial objects	B'nai Brith Library	70
Near Eastern paintings	Freer Gallery	18
Oriental Rugs	Textile Museum	76
Peacock Room/Paintings — James McNeil Whistler	Freer Gallery	18
Pre-Columbian Art	Dumbarton Oaks	76
Religious mosaics	Shrine Immaculate Con	52
Stradivarius violins & antique musical instruments	Freer Gallery	18

HISTORICAL

Bible of Mainz — (1453)	Library of Congress	16
Bill of Rights	Archives	16
Congress Bells — replica of Westminster 1596 bells	Old Post Office	16
Constitution of the United States of America	Archives	16
Declaration of Independence — First draft	Library of Congress	16
Early maps	Library of Congress	16
Elizabethan theater	Folger Library	18
First Ladies' ball gowns	Museum American History	18
Gutenberg Bible — (1455)	Library of Congress	16
Lincoln's Gettysburg Address — 1st & 2nd drafts	Library of Congress	16
Matthew Brady photographs	Library of Congress	16
Presidents' papers: Washington, Jefferson, Lincoln, Wilson	Lib Congrss	16
Revolutionary War memorabilia	Anderson House	76
Shakespeare first folios	Folger Library	18
Star Spangled Banner (original)	Mus American History	18
United Nations Charter	Archives	16

SCIENTIFIC

Antique guns	National Rifle Assoc	76
Aquarium — 2,000 species exotic fish	National Aquarium	76
Atomic clock	Naval Observatory	76
Benjamin Franklin's printing press	Mus of American History	18
Edison's electric lamp	Mus of American History	18
Earlybird satellite	Air & Space Museum	18
Foucault pendulum	Mus of American History	18
Gems — Hope Diamond, Star of Asia Sapphire	Mus Natural History	18
Kitty Hawk Flyer — Wright Brothers	Air & Space Museum	18
Lunar Rock	Air & Space Museum	18
Space Craft — Friendship 7, Apollo II, Discoverer 13	Air & Space	18
Spirit of St Louis	Air & Space Museum	18

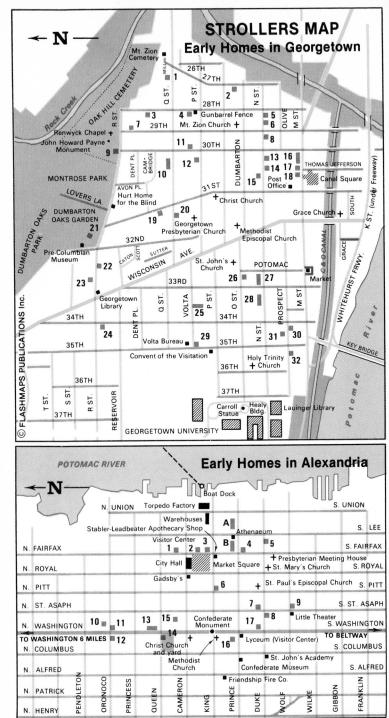

STROLLERS MAP
Early Homes in Georgetown

← N →

Mt. Zion Cemetery

OAK HILL CEMETERY

Rock Creek

Renwyck Chapel
John Howard Payne Monument

MONTROSE PARK

LOVERS LA.

DUMBARTON OAKS GARDEN

DUMBARTON OAKS PARK

Pre-Columbian Museum

© FLASHMAPS PUBLICATIONS Inc.

MILL ST

Q ST

P ST

R ST

26TH
27TH
28TH

29TH

30TH

DENT PL
CAM-BRIDGE

AVON PL
Hurt Home for the Blind

31 ST

32ND

CATON
SCOTT
SUTTER

WISCONSIN AVE.

33RD

34TH

35TH

DENT PL

Q ST
VOLTA
P ST
O ST

Georgetown Library

Volta Bureau

Convent of the Visitation

36TH
37TH

T ST
S ST
R ST
RESERVOIR

N ST

Gunbarrel Fence
Mt. Zion Church ✝

OLIVE ST
M ST

DUMBARTON

THOMAS JEFFERSON
Canal Square

Post Office

Christ Church ✝

Grace Church ✝

Georgetown Presbyterian Church

Methodist Episcopal Church ✝

St. John's Church ✝

POTOMAC

Market

N ST
PROSPECT
M ST

34TH

N ST

Holy Trinity ✝ Church

35TH

36TH

37TH

Carroll Statue
Healy Bldg.
Lauinger Library

GEORGETOWN UNIVERSITY

SOUTH
GRACE

K ST (under Freeway)

WHITEHURST FRWY.

C & O CANAL

Potomac River

KEY BRIDGE

1 2 3 4 5 6 7 8 9 10 11 12 13 14 15 16 17 18 19 20 21 22 23 24 25 26 27 28 29 30 31 32

Early Homes in Alexandria

POTOMAC RIVER

← N →

Boat Dock

Torpedo Factory

Warehouses

Stabler-Leadbeater Apothecary Shop

N. UNION
S. UNION

N. FAIRFAX

Visitor Center

City Hall

Gadsby's

N. ROYAL

N. PITT

N. ST. ASAPH

N. WASHINGTON

TO WASHINGTON 6 MILES

N. COLUMBUS

N. ALFRED

N. PATRICK

N. HENRY

PENDLETON
ORONOCO
PRINCESS
QUEEN
CAMERON
KING
PRINCE
DUKE
WOLF
WILKE
GIBBON
FRANKLIN

Athenaeum

Market Square

Presbyterian Meeting House ✝
St. Mary's Church ✝

St. Paul's Episcopal Church ✝

Little Theater

Confederate Monument

Lyceum (Visitor Center)

Christ Church and yard ✝

Methodist Church

St. John's Academy
Confederate Museum

Friendship Fire Co.

TO BELTWAY →

S. LEE
S. FAIRFAX
S. ROYAL
S. PITT
S. ST. ASAPH
S. WASHINGTON
S. COLUMBUS
S. ALFRED

A B 1 2 3 4 5 6 7 8 9 10 11 12 13 14 15 16 17

66

GEORGETOWN HOUSES—BY MAP NUMBER

Map No.	House	Address	Architect	Date
1	Dumbarton House	2715 Q	Benjamin Latrobe	1805
2	Trentman House	1350 27th	H. N. Jacobsen	1968
3	Evermay	1628 28th	Nicholas King	1801
4	Miller House	1524 28th	Benjamin Miller	1840
5	Gannt-Williams House	2806 N	Unknown	1817
6	Decatur House	2812 N	J. S. Williams	1813
7	Mackall Square	1633 29th	Benjamin Mackall	1820
8	Foxall House	2908 N	Henry Foxall	c1820
9	Oak Hill Cem Gatehouse	30th & R	de la Roche	1850
10	Cooke's Row	3007-29 Q	Starkweather-Plowman	1868
11	Francis Dodge House	1517 30th	Downing & Vaux	1852
12	Linthicum House	3019 P	Edward Linthicum	1829
13	Laird-Dunlop House	3014 N	William Lovering	1799
14	Riggs-Riley House	3038 N	Romulus Riggs	1816
15	Wheatley House	3041-43 N	Francis Wheatley	1859
16	Thomas Sim Lee Corner	3001-9 M	Unknown	1794
17	Loughboro-Patterson	3039-41 N	Unknown	1801
18	Old Stone House	3051 M	Christopher Layhman	1766
19	Tudor Place	1644 31st	Dr. Wm. Thornton	1815
20	Bowie-Sevier House	3124 Q	Washington Bowie	1805
21	Dumbarton Oaks	3101 R	William H. Dorsey	1801
22	Scott-Grant House	3238 R	A.V. Scott	1858
23	Dougall House	3259 R	Adams & Haskins	1854
24	Mackall-Worthington	1686 34th	Leonard Mackall	1820
25	Pomander Walk	Volta Place	Unknown	1885
26	Bodisco House	3222 O	Clement Smith	1815
27	Smith Row	3255-63 N	W. & C. Smith	1815
28	Cox's Row	3327-39 N	John Cox	1817
29	Alexander Melville Bell	1525 35th	Unknown	c1850
30	Halcyon House	3400 Prospect	Benjamin Stoddert	1787
31	"Quality Hill"	3425 Prospect	J.T. Mason	1798
32	Prospect House	3508 Prospect	J. M. Lingan	1788

EARLY ALEXANDRIA HOUSES—BY MAP NUMBER

Map No.	House	Address	Date
1	Thompson-Marshburn House	211 N Fairfax	1799
2	Carlyle House	121 N Fairfax	1752
3	Ramsay House	King & Fairfax	1749
4	Dr. William Brown House	212 S. Fairfax	1775
5	Dr. James Craik House	210 Duke	1789
6	Marshall House	King & Pitt	c1850
7	Dulaney House	601 Duke	1785
8	Lawrason-Lafayette House	Duke & S. St. Asaph	1820
9	Vowell-Smith House	Wolfe & S. St. Asaph	1840
10	Robert E. Lee House	607 Oronoco	1795
11	Fendall-John L. Lewis House	614 Oronoco	c1800
12	Edmund Jennings Lee House	Oronoco & N. Wash.	1800
13	Brockett's Row	301-7 N. Wash.	1840
14	Lloyd House	Queen & N. Wash.	c1793
15	Yeaton-Fairfax House	607 Cameron	1799
16	William Fowle House	711 Prince	c1800
17	Lloyd's Row	220-28 S. Wash.	1811

A. B. Captain's Row & Prince Street Row Houses, 18th Century

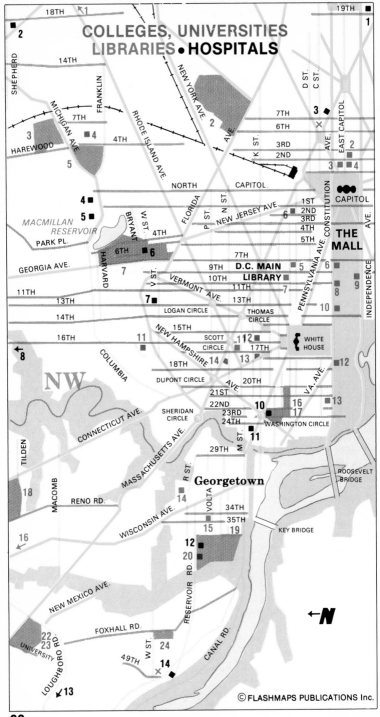

COLLEGES, UNIVERSITIES
LIBRARIES • HOSPITALS

18TH

19TH

2

1

SHEPHERD

14TH

FRANKLIN

NEW YORK AVE.

D ST.
C ST.

3

7TH
6TH

2

MICHIGAN AVE.

7TH

RHODE ISLAND AVE.

EAST CAPITOL

3

4

HAREWOOD

3

4TH

K ST.

3RD
2ND

3

4

5

NORTH   CAPITOL.

CONSTITUTION

CAPITOL

4

BRYANT

W ST.

FLORIDA

P ST.

N ST.

NEW JERSEY AVE.

1ST
2ND
3RD
4TH
5TH

THE
MALL

MACMILLAN
RESERVOIR

5

6

PARK PL.

4TH

PENNSYLVANIA AVE. CONSTITUTION

6

INDEPENDENCE

GEORGIA AVE.

HARVARD

6TH

6

7TH

D.C. MAIN
LIBRARY

5

7

V ST.

9TH
10TH

8

9

11TH

VERMONT AVE.

11TH

7

13TH

13TH

10

LOGAN CIRCLE

THOMAS
CIRCLE

7

14TH

15TH

SCOTT
CIRCLE

12

WHITE
HOUSE

16TH

11

NEW HAMPSHIRE

17TH

14

13

12

8

NW

COLUMBIA

18TH

DUPONT CIRCLE

AVE.

20TH

VA. AVE.

13

CONNECTICUT AVE.

SHERIDAN
CIRCLE

21ST
22ND
23RD
24TH

M ST.

10

16

17

WASHINGTON CIRCLE

11

TILDEN

MASSACHUSETTS AVE.

29TH

ROOSEVELT
BRIDGE

MACOMB

RENO RD.

18

R ST.

Georgetown

VOLTA

14

16

WISCONSIN AVE.

34TH
35TH

15

19

KEY BRIDGE

N

12

20

NEW MEXICO AVE.

RESERVOIR RD.

CANAL RD.

22
23

FOXHALL RD.

24

UNIVERSITY RD.

LOUGHBORO RD.

49TH

W ST.

14

13

© FLASHMAPS PUBLICATIONS Inc.

68

HOSPITALS•COLLEGES•LIBRARIES—BY MAP NO.

HOSPITALS
1 DC General
2 Hosp Sick Children
3 Capitol Hill
4 Veteran's Admin
5 Washington Center
6 Freedman's
7 Children's
8 Walter Reed
10 GWU Medical Ctr
11 Columbia
12 Georgetown
13 Sibley Hospital
14 Psychiatric

COLLEGES
2 Gallaudet College
3 Catholic University
4 St. Paul's College

5 Trinity College
6 Georgetown Law
7 Howard University
11 Antioch Schl Law
12 Benjamin Franklin
13 Berlitz School
14 Johns Hopkins
16 GWU Medical
17 Geo Washington U
17 GWU Schl Engr
18 Univ of DC
19 Georgetown Univ
20 Georgetown Dentist
20 Georgetown Med
20 G'twn Schl Nursing
22 American University
23 Wesley Theolog
24 Mt Vernon College

LIBRARIES
1 Nat'l Agricultural
2 Folger Shakespeare
3 Supreme Court
4 Library of Congress
5 National Collection
6 National Archives
7 Martin Luth King
8 Natural History
9 Arts & Industries
10 Hist & Technology
11 Board Education
11 B'nai Brith
12 Org Amer States
13 Natl Acad Sciences
14 Dumbarton Oaks
15 Volta Bureau
16 Nat'l Lib Medicine

HOSPITALS•COLLEGES•LIBRARIES

HOSPITAL

	Address	Map No.	Telephone
Capitol Hill	700 Constitution Ave NE	3	269-8000
Children's Hospital	111 Michigan Ave NW	7	745-5000
Columbia Hospital for Women	2425 L St NW	11	293-6500
DC General	Mass Ave & 19th St SE	1	675-5000
Geo Washington Univ Med Ctr	901 23rd St NW	10	676-6000
Georgetown University	3800 Reservoir Rd	12	625-0100
Greater Southeast Community	1310 Southern Ave SE	★	574-6000
Hadley	4601 Martin Luther King SW	★	574-5700
Hospital for Sick Children	1731 Bunker Hill Rd	2	832-4400
Howard University	2041 Georgia Ave NW	6	865-6100
Providence	1150 Varnum NE	★	269-7000
Psychiatric Institute	4460 Mac Arthur Blvd NW	14	944-3400
Sibley	5255 Loughboro Rd NW	13	537-4000
St. Elizabeth's	Congress Heights	★	562-4000
Veteran's Administration	50 Irving NW	4	745-8000
Walter Reed	6825 16th St NW	8	545-6700
Washington Hospital Center	110 Irving NW	5	541-0500

COLLEGE/UNIVERSITY

	Address	Map No.	Telephone
American University	Mass & Nebraska NW	22	686-2000
Antioch School of Law	1624 Crescent Pl NW	11	265-9500
Benjamin Franklin Univ	1100 Sixteenth NW	12	994-1000
Berlitz School of Languages	1050 Connecticut Ave NW	13	331-1160
Catholic Univ of America	620 Michigan NE	3	635-5000
Gallaudet College	Florida & 7th St NE	2	651-5000
George Washington Univ	2121 1st St NW	17	676-6000
GWU School of Engineering	801 22nd Street NW	17	994-6083
GWU School of Medicine	2300 Eye St NW	16	676-6000
Georgetown University	O & 37th St NW	19	687-0100
Georgetown Law Center	600 New Jersey NW	6	662-9000
Georgetown School Dentistry	3900 Reservoir Road NW	20	687-5055
Georgetown School of Med	3900 Reservoir Road NW	20	687-0100
Georgetown School of Nursing	3700 Reservoir Road NW	20	687-0100

★ off map

69

HOSPITALS•COLLEGES•LIBRARIES—Continued

COLLEGE/UNIVERSITY	Address	Map No.	Telephone
Howard University	2400 6th St NW	7	636-6100
Johns Hopkins Internat'l Univ	1740 Mass Ave NW	14	663-5600
Mount Vernon College	2100 Foxhall Rd NW	24	331-0400
National War College	Fort McNair	off	545-6700
St. Paul's College	3015 4th St NE	4	832-6262
Trinity College	Michigan & Franklin St NE	5	939-5000
University of D.C.	4200 Conn NW	18	282-7300
Wesley Theological Institute	4500 Mass Ave NW	23	885-8600

LIBRARY

	Address	Map No.	Telephone
Arts and Industries	The Mall	9	357-1300
Board of Ed Sumner Research	17th & M Street NW	11	727-3419
B'nai B'rith "Four Freedoms"	1640 Rhode Island NW	11	857-6600
Collection of Fine Arts	G St & 8th NW	5	357-1300
Dumbarton Oaks Garden	1703 32nd St NW	14	342-3240
Folger Shakespeare	201 East Capitol	2	544-4600
History and Technology	The Mall	10	357-1300
Library of Congress	10 1st St SE & Independ	4	707-5000
Martin Luther King Memorial	901 G St NW	7	727-1111
National Academy Sciences	2101 Constitution NW	13	334-2000
National Agricultural	Beltsville, Maryland	1	*344-3755
National Archives	Penn Ave & 8th St NW	6	523-3220
National Library of Medicine	600 Rockville Pk, Rockville	16	*496-6095
Natural History	The Mall	8	357-1300
Organization American States	Constitution & 17th St NW	12	458-3000
Supreme Court	1st St & Maryland NE	3	479-3175
Volta Bureau	1537 35th St NW	15	337-5220

★ Area (301)

MAJOR STORES IN SHOPPING CENTERS (Map Page 71)

CHEVY CHASE / MAZZA—WOODWARD & LOTHROP, LORD & TAYLOR, SAKS FIFTH AVE, GUCCI NEIMAN MARCUS, ANN TAYLOR, F A O SCHWARZ, SAINT-LAURENT, CHAS SCHWARTZ

DOWNTOWN DC—GARFINCKEL'S, LORD & TAYLOR, BURBERRY'S, ARTHUR ADLER, HECHT'S, RALEIGHS, CASUAL CORNER, ARTHUR ASHE TENNIS, S. KLEIN, MORTON'S, JAEGER'S THE PAVILION - 30 SPECIALTY SHOPS, THE SHOPS AT NATIONAL PLACE - 85 SHOPS INTERNATIONAL SQ - 30 STORES, METROPOLITAN SQ - 20 STORES, UNION STATION - 35 STORES

GEORGETOWN—THE PHOENIX, GEORGETOWN LEATHER DESIGN, THE FRENCH SHOP, BRITCHES, PAPPAGALLO, ANN TAYLOR, DOROTHY STEAD, SAINT-AUBIN, GEORGETOWN UNIVERSITY SHOP GEORGETOWN PARK - 100 RETAIL SHOPS

LANDMARK—HECHT'S, SEARS, RALEIGHS, CASUAL CORNER, GEORGETOWN LEATHER DESIGN

LANDOVER—GARFINCKEL'S, WOODWARD & LOTHROP, SEARS, HECHT'S, GORDONS, RALEIGHS CASUAL CORNER, SEVEN & NINE, BAILEY BANKS & BIDDLE, B. DALTON, KAY JEWELERS

MONTGOMERY—GARFINCKEL'S, WOODWARD & LOTHROP, SCANDINAVIAN COLLECTION, SEARS, HECHT'S, BAILEY BANKS & BIDDLE, CAMALIER & BUCKLEY, BRITCHES, RALEIGHS

PRINCE GEORGE—WOODWARD & LOTHROP, HECHT'S, RALEIGHS, WILSONS, MURPHYS, UPS N' DOWNS, LANE BRYANT, IRVIN'S SPORT, THE LIMITED, WOOLWORTH'S

SEVEN CORNERS—GARFINCKEL'S, WOODWARD & LOTHROP, W. & J. SLOANE, LERNERS

SPRINGFIELD—GARFINCKEL'S, RALEIGHS, MONTGOMERY WARD, J.C. PENNEY, BRITCHES, YOUNG FAIR, PHILIPS, CASUAL CORNER, GEORGETOWN LEATHER, B.DALTON, THE LIMITED

TYSON'S CORNER—GARFINCKEL'S, WOODWARD & LOTHROP, BLOOMINGDALE'S, HECHT'S ANN TAYLOR, GEORGETOWN LEATHER, CRABTREE & EVELYN, RALEIGHS, B, BANKS & BIDDLE

WATERGATE—AFAF BOUTIQUE, ST. LAURENT, VALENTINO, COLETTE, SAKS-JANDEL, GUCCI

WHITE FLINT—BLOOMINGDALE'S, LORD & TAYLOR, I. MAGNIN, ALFRED DUNHILL, SAINT LAURENT RALEIGHS, CRABTREE & EVELYN, BLACK STAR & FROST, ANN TAYLOR, GEORGETOWN LEATHER

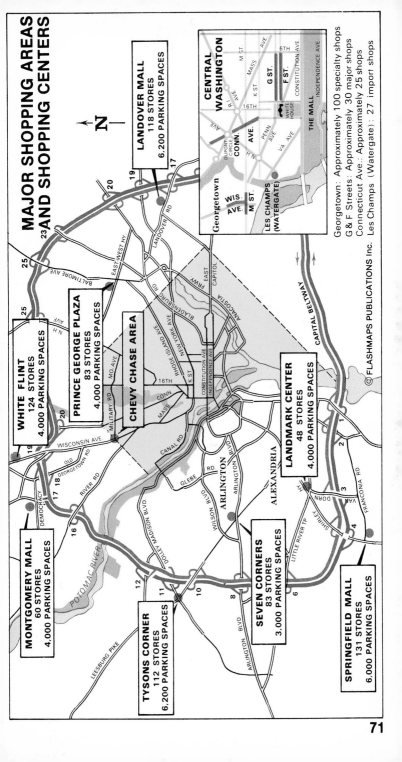

MAJOR SHOPPING AREAS AND SHOPPING CENTERS

LANDOVER MALL
118 STORES
6,200 PARKING SPACES

WHITE FLINT
124 STORES
4,000 PARKING SPACES

PRINCE GEORGE PLAZA
83 STORES
4,000 PARKING SPACES

CHEVY CHASE AREA

MONTGOMERY MALL
60 STORES
4,000 PARKING SPACES

TYSONS CORNER
112 STORES
6,200 PARKING SPACES

SEVEN CORNERS
83 STORES
3,000 PARKING SPACES

LANDMARK CENTER
48 STORES
4,000 PARKING SPACES

SPRINGFIELD MALL
131 STORES
6,000 PARKING SPACES

CENTRAL WASHINGTON

LES CHAMPS (WATERGATE)

THE MALL

Georgetown: Approximately 100 specialty shops
G & F Streets: Approximately 30 major shops
Connecticut Ave.: Approximately 25 shops
Les Champs (Watergate): 27 import shops

© FLASHMAPS PUBLICATIONS Inc.

71

WASHINGTON'S WEATHER

SEASON	CLIMATE	AVERAGE HIGH	AVERAGE LOW
Summer	Warm Humid	86°F	67°F
Winter	Mild	45°F	29°F
Spring	Pleasant	66°F	56°F
Fall	Ideal	69°F	50°F

Average annual rainfall 39 inches

Average annual snowfall 17 inches

Average wind speed 9 mph

Prevailing wind direction South

Growing season 194 days

Mean daily relative humidity 52%–73%

Sunshine 60% of possible total

CAPITAL CEN
EAST CAPITO
TO LARGO, M

KEI

KENILWO
AQUAT
GARDE

ICE SKATING
(IN SEASON)

NE

ANACO

BLADENSBUR

OUTDOOR POOL
TENNIS COURTS (4)

TENNIS COURTS (5)

PERRY ST
OTIS ST
SOUTH DAKOTA

NEW YORK AVE

OLIVE

GALLATIN ST

TENNIS COURTS (8)

RHODE ISLAND

MICHIGAN

BR

TENNIS COURTS (2)

HO
ICE SKA

OUTDOOR POOL
TENNIS COURTS (8)

FORT TOTEN PARK

2ND
AVE

FLORIDA

U.S. SOLDIERS
HOME

HIKING &
BIKING
TRAILS

BLAIR
NEW HAMPSHIRE
FORT TOTEN
AVE

FORT SLOCUM
PARK

TENNIS COURTS (6)
OUTDOOR POOL

KANSAS AVE

QUINCY ST

TENNIS COURTS (8)
OUTDOOR POOL

7TH
9TH

BRANCH
RD

MISSOURI
ILLINOIS

GEORGIA AVE

TENNIS COURTS (2)
INDOOR POOL

13TH
14TH

ALASKA AVE

WALTER
REED HOSP.

TENNIS COURTS
(4)

COLORADO

DECATUR ST
ALLISON ST
ARK AVE

INDOOR POOL
OUTDOOR POOL

16TH

16TH

MERIDIAN HILL
PARK

PUBLIC
GOLF COURSE

TENNIS COURTS
(22)

ROCK CREEK PKWY

UPSHUR
AVE

NW

ROCK   CREEK   PARK

ROCK CREEK

NATIONAL
ZOOLOGICAL
PARK

TENNIS COURTS

SEE ROCK CREEK PARK MAP P. 59

TENNIS COURTS (3)

TENNIS COURTS
OUTDOOR POO

SOAPSTONE
VALLEY
PARK

PORTER
AVE

MELVIN
HAZEN
PARK

WOODLEY

TENNIS COURTS (4)

MONTROS
PARK

UTAH AVE

33RD

CONNECTICUT

RD

TENNIS COURTS (2)
OUTDOOR POOL

TENNIS COURTS (4)

37TH

NEBRASKA AVE

TENNIS COURTS (2)

MASSACHUSETTS

RESERVOIR
RD Q ST

RENO
41ST

FORT
RENO
PARK

TENNIS COURTS
(2)

WISCONSIN

RIVER
RD

CHESAPEAKE

GLOVER ARCHBOLD PARKWAY

TENNIS COURTS (2)

FOXHALL RD.

LOUGHBORO
RD

MACARTHUR BLVD.

C &

WESTMORELAND CIRCLE

TENNIS COURTS (3)

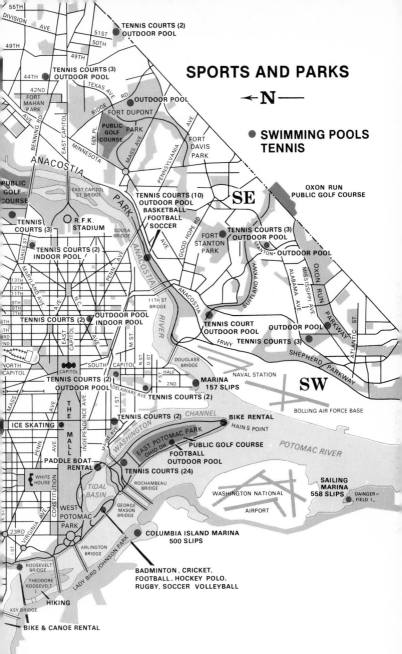

SPORTS AND PARKS

← N —

● SWIMMING POOLS
TENNIS

55TH
DIVISION AVE
49TH
51ST
50TH
TENNIS COURTS (2)
OUTDOOR POOL
44TH
42ND
TENNIS COURTS (3)
OUTDOOR POOL
FORT MAHAN PARK
TEXAS AVE RD
RIDGE PL
FORT DUPONT
OUTDOOR POOL
EAST CAPITOL
BENNING RD
ELY PL
PUBLIC GOLF COURSE
PARK
MINNESOTA
MASS AVE
PENNSYLVANIA
FORT DAVIS PARK

ANACOSTIA
PUBLIC GOLF COURSE
EAST CAPITOL ST BRIDGE
ANACOSTIA PARK
TENNIS COURTS (10)
OUTDOOR POOL
BASKETBALL
FOOTBALL
SOCCER
SE
OXON RUN
PUBLIC GOLF COURSE

TENNIS COURTS (3)
R.F.K. STADIUM
SOUSA BRIDGE
GOOD HOPE RD
FORT STANTON PARK
TENNIS COURTS (3)
OUTDOOR POOL
STANTON OUTDOOR POOL
GALES ST
TENNIS COURTS (2)
INDOOR POOL
SUTLAND PKWY
OXON RUN PARKWAY
ALABAMA AVE
MISSISSIPPI AVE
ATLANTIC ST
13TH
12TH
11TH
9TH
8TH
MARYLAND AVE
PENN AVE
N.C. AVE
ANACOSTIA RIVER
11TH ST BRIDGE
ANACOSTIA
TH
RD
ND
TENNIS COURTS (2)
OUTDOOR POOL
INDOOR POOL
EAST CAPITOL
M ST
O ST
FRWY
TENNIS COURT
OUTDOOR POOL
TENNIS COURTS (3)
OUTDOOR POOL
SHEPHERD PARKWAY

NORTH CAPITOL
SOUTH CAPITOL
DOUGLASS BRIDGE
NAVAL STATION
SW
HALF
2ND
P ST
TENNIS COURTS (2)
OUTDOOR POOL
CAPITOL
DELAWARE AVE
TENNIS COURTS (2)
MARINA
157 SLIPS
BOLLING AIR FORCE BASE
MASS AVE
PENN AVE
THE MALL
INDEPENDENCE AVE
I ST
MAINE AVE
CHANNEL
WASHINGTON
TENNIS COURTS (2)
BIKE RENTAL
HAINS POINT
POTOMAC RIVER
ICE SKATING
EAST POTOMAC PARK
OHIO DR
PUBLIC GOLF COURSE
FOOTBALL
OUTDOOR POOL
SAILING MARINA
558 SLIPS
DAINGERFIELD I.
PADDLE BOAT RENTAL
WHITE HOUSE
ROCHAMBEAU BRIDGE
TENNIS COURTS (24)
TIDAL BASIN
WASHINGTON NATIONAL AIRPORT
CONSTITUTION AVE
VIRGINIA AVE
WEST POTOMAC PARK
GEORGE MASON BRIDGE
23RD
1ST
ROOSEVELT BRIDGE
ARLINGTON BRIDGE
COLUMBIA ISLAND MARINA
500 SLIPS
THEODORE ROOSEVELT I
LADY BIRD JOHNSON PARK
BADMINTON , CRICKET,
FOOTBALL , HOCKEY POLO,
RUGBY, SOCCER VOLLEYBALL
KEY BRIDGE
HIKING
BIKE & CANOE RENTAL

ARLINGTON

FOR C. & O. CANAL
SEE MAP P. 63

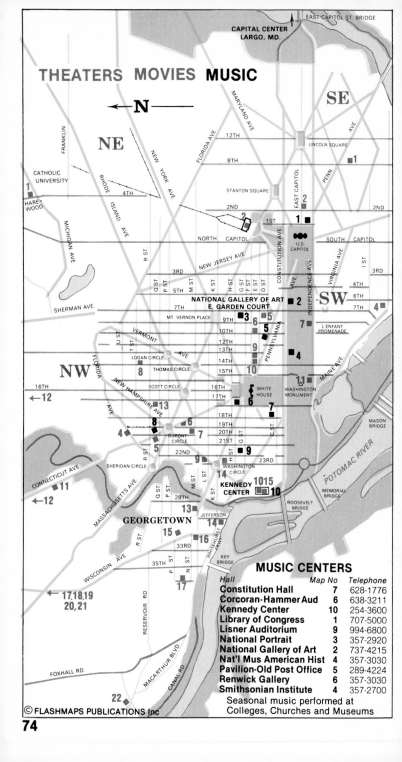

THEATERS MOVIES MUSIC

← N →

CAPITAL CENTER LARGO, MD.

SE

NE

NW

SW

GEORGETOWN

© FLASHMAPS PUBLICATIONS Inc

MUSIC CENTERS

Hall	Map No	Telephone
Constitution Hall	7	628-1776
Corcoran-Hammer Aud	6	638-3211
Kennedy Center	10	254-3600
Library of Congress	1	707-5000
Lisner Auditorium	9	994-6800
National Portrait	3	357-2920
National Gallery of Art	2	737-4215
Nat'l Mus American Hist	4	357-3030
Pavilion-Old Post Office	5	289-4224
Renwick Gallery	6	357-3030
Smithsonian Institute	4	357-2700

Seasonal music performed at
Colleges, Churches and Museums

THEATERS & MOVIES

THEATERS — ALPHABETICAL

Theater	Address	Map No	Telephone
Amer Playwrights	1742 Church NW	13	232-1122
Arena Stage	M & 6th St SW	4	488-3300
Carter Barron	16th & Kennedy	12	829-3200
dc Space	433 7th St NW	5	347-4960
Eisenhower	Kennedy Center	15	254-3670
Ford's	511 10th St NW	6	347-4833
Hartke	Harewood NE	1	529-3333
Kennedy Ctr Lab	Kennedy Center	15	857-0900
Kreeger	M & 6th St SW	4	488-3300
Marvin-Betts Center	GWU-800 21st NW	14	994-6178
National	1321 Penn NW	10	628-6161
Old Vat Room	M & 6th St SW	4	488-3300
Olney Theater	Rte 108, Olney MD	off	*924-3400
Opera House	Kennedy Center	15	254-3770
Shakespeare	Folger-201 E Capitol	2	546-4000
Smithsonian	9th & Independence	7	357-1300
Source Co,The	1809 14th St NW	8	462-1073
Studio	1333 P St NW	3	332-3300
Sylvan	The Mall	11	426-6841
Terrace Theater	Kennedy Center	15	254-9895
Trinity	36th & O St NW	17	965-4680
Warehouse Rep	1835 14th St NW	8	232-8011
Warner	513 13th St NW	9	626-1050
Wash Project Arts	400 7th St NW	5	347-8304

*Area (301)

— BY MAP NOS.

Map No	Theater
1	Hartke
2	Shakespeare
3	Studio
4	Arena Stage
4	Kreeger
4	Old Vat Rm
5	dc Space
5	Wash Proj
6	Ford's
7	Smithsonian
8	Warehouse
8	Source Co
9	Warner
10	National
11	Sylvan
12	Carter Barron
13	Amer Playwri
14	Marvin Betts
15	Eisenhower
15	Kennedy Lab
15	Opera
15	Terrace
17	Trinity

MOVIES — ALPHABETICAL

Movie	Address	Map No	Telephone
AMC Union Station 9	Union Station	2	842-3751
Amer Film Institute	Kennedy Center	10	785-4600
Avalon I, II	5612 Conn NW	12	966-2600
Biograph	2819 M St NW	13	333-2696
Capitol Hill I, II	507 8th St SE	1	547-1210
Cerberus 1, 2, 3	3040 M St NW	14	337-1311
Cinema	5120 Wis NW	18	363-1875
Cineplex Dupont 5	Conn at 19th NW	6	872-9556
Cineplex Embassy	1927 Florida NW	4	387-1344
Cineplex Jeniferl,II	5252 Wis NW	17	244-5703
Cine MacArthur 1-3	4859 MacArthur	22	337-1700
Cineplex Outer I, II	4849 Wis NW	19	244-3116
Cineplex Tenley I-III	4200 Wis NW	21	363-4340
Cineplex Uptown	3426 Conn NW	11	966-5400
Cine West End 1-4	23rd & L St NW	9	293-3152
Cine West End 5-7	23rd & M St NW	9	452-9020
Cineplex Wisconsin 5	4000 Wis NW	21	244-0880
Fine Arts	1919 M St	7	223-4438
Georgetown	1351 Wis NW	15	333-5555
Janus 1, 2,3	1660 Conn NW	5	232-8900
KB Foundry 7	1055 Thos Jefferson	14	337-0094
Key	1222 Wis NW	16	333-5100
Paris 1-3	5300 Wis NW	18	686-7700
Studio I, II, III	4600 Wis NW	20	686-1700

— BY MAP NOS.

Map No	Theater
1	Capitol
2	AMC Union Sta
4	Cine Embassy
5	Janus 1, 2, 3
6	Cine Dupont
7	Fine Arts
9	Cine West 1-4
9	Cine West 5-7
10	Amer Film Inst
11	Cine Uptown
12	Avalon I,II
13	Biograph
14	Cerberus 1-3
14	KB Foundry 7
15	Georgetown
16	Key
17	Cine Jenifer
18	Cinema
18	Paris
19	Cine Outer
20	Studio
21	Cine Tenley
21	Cine Wisconsin
22	Cine MacArthur

Wolf Trap Farm 1624 Trap Rd, Vienna, VA (703) 255-1800 (see page 61)

MUSEUMS—ART • HISTORY • SCIENCE

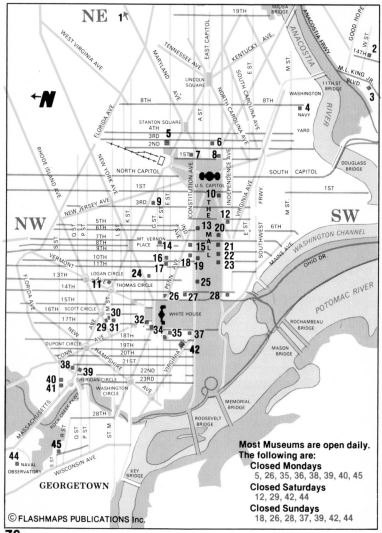

Most Museums are open daily.
The following are:
Closed Mondays
5, 26, 35, 36, 38, 39, 40, 45
Closed Saturdays
12, 29, 42, 44
Closed Sundays
18, 26, 28, 37, 39, 42, 44

© FLASHMAPS PUBLICATIONS Inc.

MUSEUMS—ART • HISTORY • SCIENCE

Museum	Address	Weekday Hours ★	Map No.	Telephone
Air & Space Museum	The Mall	10-5:30	20	357-2700
Anacostia Neighborhood/Mus	1901 Fort Pl SE	10-5	3	287-3369
Anderson House	2118 Mass NW	1-4	39	785-0540
Arthur M. Sackler Asian Art	The Mall	10-5:30	22	357-2700
Arts & Industries Building	The Mall	10-5:30	22	357-2700
Bethune Archives	1318 Vermont Ave NW	11-4:30	11	332-1233
B'nai B'rith Klutznick	1640 Rhode Island NW	10-4:30	29	857-6583
Botanic Gardens	The Mall	9-5	10	225-8333
Bureau Engraving, Printing	14th & C St SW	9-2	28	566-2000
Capitol, The	The Mall	9-3:30	10	225-6827
Children's Museum	800 3rd St, NE	10-5	5	543-8600
Corcoran Gallery	17th & New York NW	10-4:30	35	638-3211
DAR Museum	1776 D St NW	8:30-4	35	628-1776
Decatur, Stephen House	748 Jackson Place	10-2	32	673-4030
Dept of Interior	C & Virginia Ave, NW	8:30-4	42	343-2743
Dolls' & Toy Museum	5236 44th St, NW	10-5	off	244-0024
Dumbarton Oaks/Gardens	1703 32nd St NW	2-5	45	338-8278
Federal Bur Investigation	Penn & 9th St NW	9-4:15	18	324-3447
Folger Shakespeare Library	201 E Capitol	10-4:30	6	544-7077
Ford's Theater	511 10th St NW	9-5	16	426-6924
Frederick Douglass Home	14th & W St SE	9-5	2	426-5960
Freer Gallery	The Mall	(temporarily closed)	23	357-2700
Hillwood Museum	4155 Linnean Ave NW	by app't	off	686-5807
Hirshhorn Mus & Sculpture	The Mall	10-5:30	21	357-2700
Howard Univ Art Gallery	2455 6th Street, NW	9-5	off	636-7070
Jewish Historic Soc/Mus	701 Third St. NW	Tue-Th	9	789-0900
Library of Congress	Independence & 1st SE	8:30-9	8	707-5000
Marine Corps Historic Ctr	9th & M SE (Navy Yd)	10-4	4	433-3534
Mus Modern Latin Amer Art	201 18th St NW	9-5	37	458-6019
National African Art	The Mall	10-5:30	22	357-2700
National American History	The Mall	10-5:30	25	357-2700
National Aquarium	14th & E St NW	9-5	27	377-2825
National Arboretum	See page 58	8-5	1	475-4815
National Archives	Constitution & 8th SE	10-5	15	523-3183
National Building Museum	441 F St NW	10-4	9	272-2448
National Gallery of Art	The Mall	10-5	13	737-4215
Nat'l Geographic Explorers	17th & M St NW	9-5	31	857-7588
National Firearms Museum	Rhode Island & 16th	10-4	30	828-6194
National Women in the Arts	801 13th Street NW	10-5	24	783-5000
National Zoo	3000 Conn (see pg 60)	9-4:30	off	673-4800
Natural History Museum	The Mall	10-5:30	19	357-2700
Naval Observatory	Mass & 34th St NW	8:00pm	44	653-1543
Navy, The	9th & MSE (Navy Yd)	9-4	4	433-2651
Octagon House	1799 New York NW	10-4	36	638-3105
Peterson House (LINCOLN DIED)	516 10th St NW	9-5	17	426-6830
Phillips Collection	1600 21st St NW	10-5	38	387-2151
Portrait Gallery/Mus Amer Art	G St & 8th NW	10-5:30	14	357-2700
Renwick Gallery	Penn & 17th St NW	10-5:30	34	357-2700
Sewall-Belmont House	144 Constitution NE	10-3	7	546-3989
Textile Museum	2320 S St NW	10-5	40	667-0441
White House	1600 Pennsylvania NW	10-12	26	456-7041
Woodrow Wilson House	2340 S St NW	10-4	41	387-4062
Voice of America	330 Independence SW	9-3	12	485-6231

★ **Hours vary Saturday, Sunday & Summer months**

WASHINGTON SUBURBS

Community/Population	Approx Miles Center DC	Routes to Area	Nearest Beltway Exit ★
Alexandria, VA (103,217)	6	Route 1	1
Andrews AFB, MD (10,064)	10	Route 4 & 5	7-11
Annadale, VA (49,524)	12.5	Little River or Columbia Pike	6
Arlington ,VA (152,599)	5	Arlington Blvd	8
Beltsville, MD (12,760)	8.5	Route 1	25
Berwyn Heights, MD (3,135)	12	Routes 201 & 1	23
Bethesda, MD (62,736)	8	Wisconsin Ave	34
Bladensburg, MD (7,691)	6.5	Bladensburg Rd	17, 20
Bowie, MD (33,695)	15	John Hanson Hwy (Rt. 50)	19
Capitol Heights, MD (3,271)	6.5	Central Ave (Rt. 332)	15
Cheverly, MD (5,751)	6.5	John Hanson Hwy (Rt. 50)	19
Chevy Chase, MD (12,232)	6	Wisconsin or Conn Avenues	33, 34
College Park, MD (23,624)	7	Route 1	25, 23
Crystal City, VA	4	Route 1	1
District Heights, MD (6,799)	7	Marlboro Pike	11
Fairfax, VA (19,390)	15	Little River Turnpike	6
Falls Church, VA (9,515)	8	Lee Highway	8, 9
Fort Belvoir, VA (7,726)	15	Route 1	1
Friendship Heights, MD	6	Wisconsin Ave	34
Gaithersburg, MD (26,424)	20	Wash Natl Pike (Rt. 270)	38, 34
Glen Echo, MD (229)	8	Mass Ave or MacArthur Blvd	41, 39
Glendale, MD (5,106)	13	Georgetown Pike (Rt. 193)	13
Greenbelt, MD (17,332)	12	Baltimore Wash Pkwy (Rt. 1)	22
Herndon, VA (11,449)	20	Leesburg Hwy (Rt. 7)	11, 12
Hillcrest Heights, MD (17,021)	7.5	Branch Ave (Rt. 5)	7
Hollywood, MD	11	Route 1	25
Hyattsville, MD (12,709)	7	Rhode Island Ave (Rt. 1)	23, 25
Kensington, MD (1,822)	8.5	Connecticut Ave	33
Kenwood, MD	6.5	River Road	39
Laurel, MD (12,103)	16	Baltimore Wash Pkwy (Rt. 1)	25
Leisure World, MD	15	Georgia Ave (Rt. 97)	31
Lewisdale, MD	7	Route 212	25
McLean, VA (35,664)	8.5	Route 123	11
Merrifield, VA (7,525)	10	Lee Highway	8, 9
Mt. Rainier, MD (7,361)	5.5	Queens Chapel Rd	25
Mt. Vernon, VA (24,058)	13	Washington Mem Hwy (Rt. 1)	1
Oxon Hill, MD (36,267)	9	Indian Head (Rt. 210)	3
Reston, VA (36,407)	18	Leesburg Pike (Rt. 7)	11, 12
Rockville, MD (43,811)	15	Rockville Pike (Rt. 355)	34
Seat Pleasant, MD (5,217)	7.5	Route 704	15, 17
Silver Spring, MD (72,893)	7	Route 29	29, 36
Somerset, MD (1,101)	6.5	Wisconsin Avenue	34
Springfield, VA (21,435)	12	Shirley Hwy (Rt. 95)	4
Suitland, MD (32,164)	6.5	Route 218	7
Takoma Park, MD (16,231)	6	Georgia Ave & Piney Branch	30, 29
Tremont, VA	9	Arlington Blvd (Rt. 50)	8
Tyson's Corner, VA (10,065)	10	Dolly Madison & Leesburg Pk	10, 11
Wheaton, MD (48,598)	10	Georgia Ave (Rt. 97)	31
Vienna, VA (15,469)	13	Route 123	10, 11
White Oak, Md (13,700)	11	Route 29	28-30

★ Beltway Map page 6

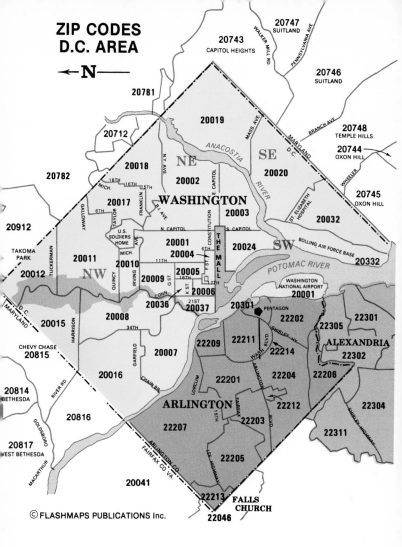

ZIP CODES
D.C. AREA
← N →

© FLASHMAPS PUBLICATIONS Inc.

General Post Office · N Capitol & M assachusetts Ave · 7am to midnight
Main Post Office · 200 Brentwood Rd NE · 8am to 8pm

ZIP CODE INFORMATION:

682-9595 · weekdays 7:00 am to 12 pm

The White House	20500
The Senate	20510
House of Representatives	20515
The Supreme Court	20543

GLOSSARY

English	French	German	Italian	Spanish
Architecture	Architecture	Architektur	Architettura	Arquitectura
Art	Art	Kunst	Arte	Arte
Buses	Autobus	Autobusse	Autobus	Autobus
Churches	Eglises	Kirchen	Chiese	Iglesias
Colleges	Universites	Universitaten	Universita'	Universidades
Embassies	Ambassades	Botschaften	Ambasciate	Embajadas
Emergency Numbers	Numeros d'urgence	Notnummern	Numeri d'emergenza	Numeros de Emergencia
Galleries	Galleries	Gallerien	Gallerie	Galeria
History	Histoire	Geschichte	Storia	Istoria
Highways	Grandes Routes	Landstrassen	Autostrade	Carreteras
Hospitals	Hopitaux	Krakenhauser	Ospedali	Hospital
Hotels	Hotels	Hotels	Hotel	Hotel
Libraries	Bibliteques	Bibliotheken	Biblioteche	Bibliotecas
Museums	Musees	Museen	Musei	Museos
Music	Musique	Musik	Musica	Musica
Movies	Cinemas	Filme	Cinema	Peliculas
Parks	Parcs	Parks	Giardini Publici	Parques
Restaurants	Restaurants	Restaurants	Ristoranti	Restaurantes
Science	Science	Wissenschaft	Scienze	Ciencia
Shops	Grands Magasins	Einkaufen	Negozi	Negocios
Sports	Sports	Sport	Sport	Desportes
Subways	Metro	Untergrundbahnen	Metropolitana	Subterraneo
Taxi	Taxi	Taxi	Tassi'	Taxi
Theaters	Theatres	Theater	Teatri	Teatros
Zoo	Zoo	Zoo	Zoo	Jardin Zoologico